Sacred Transitions
Taking a More Conscious Role with Dying

This heartwarming and enlightening story about life and death enables you to understand your true spiritual nature and how life continues beyond the physical body. Julie Milne leads you on a journey that is filled with love and understanding, forgiveness and healing. I highly recommend this book. It is informative and a story that relates to us all. Julie helps us to know that we are far more than what we perceive as physical beings, and how unconditional love can truly make a difference with our loved ones in transition.

~Kimberly Hayes Curcio, Author of *Man of Light*, President, Delphi University of Spiritual Studies

This book is a must read for everyone with aging family members. There is so much love and compassion contained in these pages. It was inspiring to read about the beautiful way that Julie's mother was cared for in her final weeks, days and hours. We may think we are prepared for the passing of a loved one, but my personal experience showed me otherwise. If I had read this book sooner, I would have handled the transition of my own mother in a completely different way. This book has inspired me to consider what I would want for myself when my time comes. I feel that I am more prepared for the final step of a sacred journey... for myself and those I love.

~Carol A. Lampman, Director, Integration Concepts

Reading Sacred Transitions had an influence on the quality of my time with my father in the final months before his passing. At the time of his death, there was an atmosphere of great peace and love. I was present to the great privilege in being witness to his stepping across. I am so grateful to Julie Milne for telling her story with such courage and sensitivity. It is a gift to every family who wants to be fully present in love, and even joy leading up to, and at the time of a loved-one's transition.

~Louise Northcutt, MS, Human Development Teacher, Clinical Hypnotherapist

Sacred Transitions is a must read for anyone who works with the terminally ill or who's loved one is in the end stage of life. The book would serve as a wonderful reference book for any shelf in a Hospice facility as well as communities at large. This book has a beginning, middle, and end, and Dr. Milne's writing reflects how the end with peace and love IS the beginning.

~Sally Valentine, PhD, FAACS, LCSW, Advanced Certified Hypnotherapist

SACRED TRANSITIONS

Taking a More Conscious Role with Dying

Julie M. Milne, PhD

The opinions expressed in this manuscript are solely the opinions of the author and do not represent the opinions or thoughts of the publisher. The author has represented and warranted full ownership and/or legal right to publish all the materials in this book.

Sacred Transitions
Taking a More Conscious Role with Dying
All Rights Reserved.
Copyright © 2012 Julie M. Milne, PhD
v3.0

Cover Photo © 2012 JupiterImages Corporation. All rights reserved - used with permission.

This book may not be reproduced, transmitted, or stored in whole or in part by any means, including graphic, electronic, or mechanical without the express written consent of the publisher except in the case of brief quotations embodied in critical articles and reviews.

Outskirts Press, Inc.
http://www.outskirtspress.com

ISBN: 978-1-4327-9505-4

Library of Congress Control Number: 2012911078

Outskirts Press and the "OP" logo are trademarks belonging to Outskirts Press, Inc.

PRINTED IN THE UNITED STATES OF AMERICA

Dedication

To my parents whose love brought me life
And to my spiritual and physical teachers and guides
Who helped me learn how to live it joyfully and fully.

Table of Contents

Introduction .... *ix*

Part 1: The Journey into Death as Rebirth
Chapter 1: A Promise Made 1
Chapter 2: Time Marches On: Mom's Health Declines 8
Chapter 3: A New Home but the Same Self 14
Chapter 4: Falling Down and Moving Up 20
Chapter 5: Another Fall, One Last Move 34
Chapter 6: Creating and Holding a Sacred Space
for Mom to Transition 46
Chapter 7: Giving and Receiving Love, Peace, Joy,
and Harmony 59
Chapter 8: Into the Light 79
Chapter 9: Conscious, Deliberate Closure 83

Part 2: A Handbook for Family, Friends and Caregivers
Chapter 10: Deathbed Promises and Books to Help
Prepare You for the Death and Dying
Experience 95
Chapter 11: Intention, "The Five Wishes," and
Life Review 99
Chapter 12: About Vibration, Thoughts and Words 105

Chapter 13: Staying Positive in the Face of Alzheimer's Disease, Illness, Pain, Anxiety and Fear 109
Chapter 14: The Facts About Terminal Dehydration 115
Chapter 15: Tools to Clear Space at Home or in a Health Care Setting 117
Chapter 16: Cleansing and Illuminating All Seven Chakras 128
Chapter 17: Self Care for the Caretakers 131
Chapter 18: The End-of-Life Life Review 134

Afterward *136*
Acknowledgments *139*
About the Author *140*
Bibliography *141*
Index *145*

Introduction

Imagine facing death (your own, a loved one, patient, or client's) with fear, panic, anger, and resentment. Now, imagine being faced with death coming from a place of peace, calm, acceptance, harmony, freedom, joy, integrity, and gratitude! There are many people who are choosing to cross over or transition at this time, and how they live the last months, weeks, days, and moments of their life can help determine the ease and grace with which they move into the Light. Whether they are conscious or unconscious, as in a coma, or have dementia or Alzheimer's disease, we as loved ones, health care workers or metaphysicians can help them make their transition in an atmosphere of peace, love, calmness, acceptance, freedom, and gratitude.

How each individual gets to that state of transition and where they perceive they will be after the transition varies with life circumstances, culture, and religious and spiritual beliefs. This book is the story of the journey that I took with my mother, with an emphasis on the last ten months of her life. It is a love story about a great exploration that we as two souls took together to open a way for Mom's soul to pass from one realm of life into another, thus the term transition.

The life cycle is a series of births and deaths. We are always moving from one experience to another. Over time there are people, places and things that leave our lives and are replaced with new. When we understand this cycle, we see that we are always living and dying whether it is in the physical, emotional or spiritual realms. Depending on which realm we are in, we are always crossing a threshold, transitioning either into death or birth at the same time. Death on the Earth plane is birth in the Spirit realm, and birth into the Earth plane can be a challenging transition for the soul coming from the Spirit realm. This is an account of how I helped my mother cross the threshold or transition from the Earth plane into the Spirit realm in a conscious and sacred manner.

It's also a story about building trust—my mother trusting me, trusting my connection with God (Source, Universal Field of Oneness, whatever name you use), God working through me, and me trusting my intuition. It is my hope that in sharing our story it will inspire others to pay attention to the words, shared thoughts, and behaviors of their loved ones and to be aware of struggles with mental, emotional, physical, and/or spiritual pain that may be preventing the person from knowing and feeling their connection with God and/or prolonging the suffering in preparing for one's death.

This is a personal account of how I used the gifts and knowledge I learned through meditation, prayer, personal, spiritual and metaphysical study, personal/spiritual growth work, taking subtle energy courses, studying the Bardo, and becoming certified as a Reiki Master and then a Reiki Phowa Practitioner. Reiki is a healing modality that uses life force energy. Phowa is using Reiki for helping those who are dying, or those who have died, make their transition into the Light, which is when the soul leaves the physical body and transcends to a higher level of consciousness, to unconditional love, to being with God. "God is light" (1 John 1:5).

Every moment of our lives there are biological, emotional, psychological, and spiritual aspects of ourselves that are dying and being reborn or transformed. It's part of nature's normal cycle. Death is simply another part of nature's transformation process, such as the metamorphosis of the caterpillar into the butterfly. Perennial flowers and deciduous trees grow and bloom in the spring and summer then let go of the dying flowers and leaves in the autumn and winter. But when spring returns, there is rebirth in the return of the trees' leaf buds and the tiny sprouts coming through the soil that will soon be beautiful bloom covered plants.

We get to make the choice about what we want to let go of and how we want to co-create those parts of ourselves with Source, God, whomever or whatever you honor as spiritual connection. Knowing that with each breath we are one breath closer to making the transition into the Light, it would be incredible to always have the intention of creating sacred space around ourselves—a sacred space of energy or vibration around and through ourselves that fills us with peace, love, harmony, and oneness. As Mohandas Gandhi said, "Where love is, there God is also." Neale Donald Walsch says that love dissolves fear into Feeling Excited And Ready. Creating a sacred space that is holy and safe for one who is seriously ill or dying encourages the soul to have a loving, peaceful journey when it leaves the physical body.

Many people shy away from talking about dying and death perhaps because they associate death with suffering, fear, torment, and pain. But what if humanity as a whole could be re-educated to see dying and death as the soul transitioning into the next phase of its existence? What if we saw dying as an amazing opportunity to create sacred space for the soul transitioning into the spiritual realm? What if we saw dying as a gift to heal wounded relationships, to forgive, and to love? What if we spent just as much time and took as much love, wisdom, care, and gentleness in preparing for the transition out of the physical body as we do to prepare for the birth of the soul as it enters into physical form? Just as we joyfully prepare for the birth of a new baby, we have the opportunity to put aside our judgments, fears, and grievances so that we can lovingly and graciously prepare a person to release the soul from the physical body that has cared for and provided a home for all the lessons it learned in this lifetime. Like midwives who often assist at the birth of babies, we can be midwives consciously assisting the dying to transition with grace and ease. We can make the choice about what we want for ourselves and/or we can help others prepare with excitement, joy, peace, and calm for birth into the Light.

Intentionally creating an environment with a higher vibration assists the person who is transitioning to find internal peace, forgiveness, compassion, trust, and love and helps them to ultimately let go of their physical body. My hope is that by sharing my story of consciously creating and holding a sacred space to help my mother through the last six months of her life, and especially with transitioning into the Light during the last thirteen days of her life, it will help and guide and empower the reader to deliberately create a peaceful, loving space, not only for their loved one who is departing, but for all those who share the space with the person who is transitioning.

This book is divided into two parts. The first part is the story, The Journey into Death as Rebirth, and the second part, A Handbook for Family, Friends and Caregivers, provides additional helpful and experiential information to guide and teach you about creating sacred space and caring for yourself and others through the transition process.

My experience is that being consciously present with someone while they are transitioning is beautiful, peaceful, loving, and joyful, and is one of the greatest gifts given and received.

Rosa's Radiant Transition

When the timing is right, my darling holds me (and others at her bedside) in a steady gaze, that communicates a depth of compassion, grace and love that there are no words for. Last night this became so strong for those of us sitting with her, we all felt deeply healed.

The atmosphere in the room is refined and radiant, complete with orchids, sacred music, mantras, art, and of course the view of the sunny Rockies. We read to her periodically as well and talk to her quite a bit, as she still is aware although not as much as a few days ago. Rosa's gaze continues to be radiant.

This morning at 9:06 Rosa completed her radiant transition. She was exceptionally peaceful and left with Carol, Mark and I holding her. I am so thankful that she was able to leave in this gentle way while she remained in all of your thoughts, prayers and positive energy.

Excerpts from Cam's emails April, 2012

Unconditional Love
Elizabeth Kubler-Ross, M.D. (1926-2004)
(A pioneer in the death & dying movement who had her own Near Death Experience.)

Look forward to your transition.

It's the first time you will experience unconditional love.

There will be all peace and love, and all the nightmares and the turmoil you went through in your life will be like nothing.

When you make your transition you are asked two things basically:

How much love you have been able to give and receive, and how much service you have rendered.

And you will know every consequence of every deed, every thought, and every word you have ever uttered.

And that is, symbolically speaking, going through hell when you see how many chances you have missed.

But you also see how a nice act of kindness has touched hundreds of lives that you're totally unaware of.

So concentrate on love while you're still around, and teach your children early unconditional love.

So remember, concentrate on love, and look forward to the transition.

It's the most beautiful experience you can ever imagine.

Vayas con Dios!

(Stillwater, M. & Malkin, G. (2003). Graceful passages: A companion for living and dying. A book and music CD set. Novato, CA: New World Library, p. 37.)

PART 1

THE JOURNEY INTO DEATH AS REBIRTH

CHAPTER 1

A Promise Made

"I'm wondering why Dad is hanging on when he has so little strength and so little life force left," I said to my mom one day after a visit to the nursing home.

I was trying to start a very important conversation with her about letting go of my father. As of June 2002 Dad had been living in a nursing home for six months and was under hospice care with the diagnosis of Parkinson's disease, severe osteoporosis, and failure to thrive. By mid-June he was very emaciated—down from about 170 pounds in December at the time of the fall to between 95–98 pounds, but still, he clung to life.

"Have you told Dad you'll be okay when he dies? Have you given him your blessing to cross over?" I asked.

She shook her head. "No, I don't know if I can. I'm afraid. I don't think I'll have enough money."

"Mom, giving Dad your love and permission to transition could be the most beautiful gift you ever give him."

"I can't do it right now." Her fear and anxiety were palpable.

On one hand I understood Mom's anxiety and felt compassion for the little girl in her who grew up during the Depression and often struggled with fear of not having enough. On the other hand I felt sad watching my father struggle every day to hold on. I tried to reassure Mom that she'd always have sufficient funds, and I reminded her about the Life Care Agreement she and Dad had with the senior living organization they bought into in 1998. My parents chose this particular organization because they offered progressive care, going from independent living to assisted living to nursing home care. The Life Care Agreement provided lifetime security in the event her money ran out, by insuring she would always have a place to live and she would be cared for with income from her Social Security and Medicaid. I encouraged Mom to talk with Dad, to release him from the burden of living with physical and emotional discomfort in order to continue to provide his teacher's pension.

Dad and I had many wonderful spiritually related conversations while he was in the nursing home. We talked about forgiveness, reincarnation, and deeper meanings of life. He seemed at peace with his declining situation except for leaving Mom. Dad was very tuned into my mother's energy as I guess he would be after sixty-one years of marriage. Dad shared with me that he was worried that Mom would not have sufficient financial funds to support herself after he died. I tried to ease his fears, just as I had done with Mom. And just in case Mom didn't have a conversation with Dad to assure him she would be okay when he transitioned, I promised him that I would always take care of her. It wasn't until several years later that I realized the full impact of the deathbed promise that I made to Dad. So, part of the story began with this promise I made to my dad. I just didn't know at the time what the "care" would involve. I also didn't have the awareness of all the wonderful spiritual aspects the journey of caring for Mom would open and bring for us both.

My spiritual awareness regarding the death and dying process was just beginning with Dad's transition. As part of my graduate studies in earning a master's degree in counseling and a doctorate in health psychology, I had read a couple of Elizabeth Kubler-Ross's books on death and dying and her five emotional stages of mourning for *any* significant loss. I read books on healthy grieving. I had even read a couple of books about near-death experiences (NDE). P. M. H. Atwater defines the near-death experience (NDE) as "an intense awareness, sense, or experience of 'other worldliness,' whether pleasant or unpleasant, that happens to people who are at the edge of death. It is of such magnitude that most experiencers are deeply affected—many to the point of making significant changes in their lives afterward because of what they went through." The reports of people who have experienced NDEs are usually from people pronounced dead and then revived and returned to life who share stories about witnessing a beautiful afterlife, and as a result many report they no longer fear death.

In mid-June of 2002, a couple of weeks before my father died, he blessed me by sharing visions that he was experiencing. I believe Dad was having what are termed deathbed visions (DBV) or pre-death experiences, which are somewhat different than NDEs. People experiencing the NDEs describe being out of their body traveling, while the patients who share their DBV experiences are in their physical bodies and have visions of deceased close family members, angels or other spiritual figures such as Christ, Mother Mary, or Buddha. Dad was having visits from at least one relative "on the other side," who was coming across the veil to give him a glimpse of what "Home" was about, perhaps to let him know she was there to help him bridge the gap to the afterlife.

In one conversation Dad said, "Ruth (a cousin of Dad's who had already transitioned) came earlier today and told me that a young Japanese girl is giving a Beethoven piano concert tonight. She said I'd really enjoy it. I told her thank you, but I'm not ready to go yet." Dad was very peaceful and calm in telling me the story. I gave him a kiss and thanked him for sharing this visitation with me. Dad's conversation and behavior following the vision were normal, and it was apparent to me that this was not a hallucination but a deathbed visitation. In retrospect, I wish it had occurred to me to ask him why he wasn't ready to go yet.

A couple of days after he reported the visit about the invitation to the concert, he informed me, "Ruth came again this morning. She told me she's going to teach me to make ten kinds of lace when I get to heaven. Your mother is going to be so surprised when she gets to heaven and finds out I can make lace." Mom was an avid collector of fine lace and enjoyed researching lace, particularly Irish lace.

"I know she'll be thrilled Dad," I replied. It gave me comfort to know that he was not alone and that he had someone special to help him transition. I was grateful that Dad had the wisdom to tell me about his visits with Ruth instead of telling Mom. When I told Mom about Dad's first visit and asked who Ruth was Mom said Dad was hallucinating. I explained to her that I didn't think he was hallucinating and that this was a pre-death experience. I reminded her that my cousin Sara had reported that right before Aunt Lu died she said her mother had come for her, and I explained that Dad's visions were the same. I also explained that through my readings of accounts of deathbed visions, that Aunt Lu's experience of seeing her mother right before she died is not uncommon and that the first person to welcome us into the world may be the very same person to help us leave our physical bodies and welcome us home into the Light. That helped ease Mom's mind about Dad's vision. I never told Mom about Ruth's second visit as I wanted her to be surprised when she got to heaven and found out that Dad could make lace.

Years later after Dad died and I was doing more reading on pre-death experiences, I wished I had asked my Dad more questions about his visitations. What did Ruth look like? How did it feel to know he had a special person waiting to help him cross over? Had any other family members, angels, or spiritual beings come to visit him? If so, had he had any spiritual conversations with them?

In addition to visitations and visions there were a couple of times Dad reported seeing objects. One day he asked, "Julie, do you see that beautiful bouquet of white flowers?"

Looking over to where he pointed, I replied, "I don't see it Dad, but I know it is there. Would you describe it for me?" He then described all the types of flowers in the bouquet. They were all white flowers with some greenery mixed in and beautifully arranged.

Another day, Dad said, "My grandfather's humidor is over there. Do you see it?"

"I know it's there Dad but I can't see it. You're being blessed to see this. Do you think it's a message from your grandfather?"

"I don't know. Maybe."

Curious, I asked, "Can you tell me what the humidor looks like?"

"It's made of walnut; it's hexagonal and about twelve inches high."

Our conversation was normal before, during and after Dad described the humidor, and there was no hint that he was hallucinating. I felt in my heart that the floral bouquet and the humidor were also real, but just beyond my perception. The veil that separates man in physical form from God, or separates life from death, was lifting for Dad but not for me. I wished I'd asked him if there was significance to the floral bouquet or the humidor and if anyone was carrying the two items.

When I shared the conversations with my sister, we both thought that the bouquet and humidor visions were signs about something in the future. At least that's how we chose to interpret them. Indeed, we had the white floral bouquet made the way Dad had described it for placement in front of the altar for Dad's Mass of the Resurrection. Maybe he had given us a message that this was what he wanted. Both my parents chose to be cremated, and in the selection of urns the family viewed at the funeral home, when choosing one to hold his ashes, there was one that looked just like the humidor Dad described. Coincidence? You don't have to ask which urn was chosen.

The time I spent with Dad during the last six months of his life was very precious. Unfortunately I didn't get to be with him when he transitioned from this physical life. My husband, daughter and I were leaving for Belgrade, Yugoslavia Saturday June 29th to celebrate the marriage of our son and his wife. When I arrived at the nursing home Friday evening, June 28th I knew it was the last time I was going to see my father alive. His life force energy was slipping away. Leaving him that night was one of the most difficult things I've had to do in my life, and if it had been a regular family vacation, I would not have gone.

I had read that sometimes people choose to leave this physical world on important anniversaries. My brother Kevin had died June 30, 1945 so I wondered if Kevin might come to help Dad cross over on the anniversary of his death. I told Dad that if my brother Kevin, his mother, or anyone else from the other side came and encouraged him to go into the Light, to please go. When I knew I had to say my last good-bye, I told Dad how much I loved him and that I wanted him to be at peace. His reply was, "Thank you. You will have wonderful stories to tell us when you get home."

Dad died early Tuesday morning July 2, 2002 with my brother and sister-in-law present, though he gently and quietly slipped away when no one was watching. I received the news that night at our hotel in Belgrade. My mother, sister, brother and I had all decided that we would have a memorial service for

Dad several weeks after he passed away so that it would give us all time to gather our thoughts and make plans, and it would give friends and relatives time to make travel arrangements if they wanted to join in the celebration of Dad's life. He had touched the lives of people all over the world.

Not only did I miss my father's transition, but I also missed his cremation. In Belgrade I felt lonely and incomplete for having not been physically a part of Dad's final transition process. I speak to the physical because while I was in Belgrade I was praying that Dad would transition with peace and ease into the Light, but I was not able to be totally (emotionally, physically, or mentally) present for his death and dying experience. The gift in that absence and overwhelming loneliness was that it led me to make a decision and set the intention that I would be present to the death and dying experience for Mom, if that was what she wanted.

I share these stories about my experiences with Dad because he gave me an incredible gift in each experience. There is no way I could have known that the deathbed promise I made to him to care for my mother would lead to an amazing mystical journey for Mom and me. The pre-death visions he shared showed me how much more there is to the dying process than I ever imagined, and I made a conscious decision that I wanted to learn more about death and dying.

This led to my studying the Bardo from <u>The Tibetan Book of the Dead</u>, becoming a Reiki Phowa Practitioner, becoming certified as a Dying Consciously teacher, a Heart-Centered Hypnotherapist, a RoHun therapist, and a Breath Therapist, taking courses in subtle energy, spirituality and living and dying consciously, and increasing my own spiritual practices (meditation, prayer, chanting). These all became very important during my journey with Mom as I helped her make her own sacred transition.

CHAPTER 2

Time Marches On: Mom's Health Declines

Over the next five and a half years after Dad's death, Mom's physical, emotional, and psychological wellbeing progressively declined. I had to help her move from the two bedroom apartment she'd shared with Dad to a one bedroom apartment on the same floor and I advocated as her Power of Attorney during two hospitalizations and short stays in the nursing home. In April of 2006 Mom was diagnosed with first stage Alzheimer's disease and started taking the medication Aricept® to help prevent further cognitive decline. She was determined to maintain her independence but her vision had deteriorated so much from macular degeneration that it was difficult for her to prepare her breakfast, see when her clothes were clean or not, do her laundry, or find a pill if she dropped it. Once Mom agreed to it, I found caregivers to help her maintain her independent living situation. Her struggle with progressive depression kept her from wanting to get out of bed and participate in activities where she lived and she'd want me to call and check on her two to three times a day. I purchased her over-the counter medications, toiletry items, food and clothes and would take her out for meals or bring in food I prepared. My sister also helped by visiting Mom, getting her prescriptions and filling her medication boxes, picking up items she asked for from the store, and taking her out to eat. Over the years my brother, who lives in California, went from calling Mom every Sunday to calling her every day, and he and his wife would come in several times a year for a visit. We all rallied around Mom to support her and do everything we could to maintain the highest quality of life possible for her.

A highlight of caring for Mom and supporting her emotional and psychological well-being was organizing a reception for friends and relatives to celebrate and honor her on her 90th birthday, May 9, 2005. Being happy and being social have been found to play an important role in the emotional and physical well being of the elderly, and the birthday celebration we arranged gave Mom wonderful memories and stories to share with friends for months to come. We knew it could be her last birthday so it was all the more important that we let her know how much she meant to us all.

From the time of Dad's death in July, 2002 until the spring of 2006 the subject of death and dying had not presented itself in any of my conversations with Mom. It just so happened that right after I read Neale Donald Walsch's book, <u>Home with God: In a Life That Never Ends</u>, Mom's best friend Olga was diagnosed with cancer. Olga was given only a few months to live. She was an avid reader and I gave her a copy of the book as I thought it might give her some hope and comfort in facing her own death. In a beautiful thank you note Olga wrote to me, she said the book gave her great peace. I wanted to share about the book I gave Olga, so I read Mom some of the pages that I thought contained the main ideas Mr. Walsch and God discussed in the book about letting go of fear and about death being a merging with the Divine.

I shared with Mom that to me the passages in <u>Home with God: In a Life That Never Ends</u> essentially meant that if I choose to live in love, compassion, truth, and peace and feel connected to God, I will experience within myself that union or connection with God. That connection can be felt by praying, looking at the beauty of the sunset, watching a rambunctious kitten playing, holding a baby, or looking into someone's eyes and seeing God there. If my thought of dying is being carried into the Light by angels or having deceased loved ones come to escort me across the veil into the Light, then that is what it will be. If I picture everyone in heaven (Home) having perfect health and radiating unconditional love, then that is what it will be because that is what I expect to find there. I remember asking Mom what her concept of heaven was, how she imagined it to be. I was taken back, surprised, and saddened by her defeated body posture as she answered, "I don't think about heaven. I don't know if I'm going there."

Looking directly into her eyes I very gently asked, "Well, where do you think your soul is going?" Mom just shrugged her shoulders and looked away. Her whole energy said, I don't want to talk about this anymore. Feeling tremendous sadness and great compassion in my heart, I did not press the subject further.

But, at that moment I set the intention that, if it was in Mom's highest good, I would do what I could to help her come to truly know that it is her birth right to be reborn into the Light, to know that she is love, to feel God's love, and know God is within her each and every moment. I also set the intention that when the time was right I would describe for her visual images of what (I think) heaven is like based on my meditations and on reading the stories of many people who have had near-death experiences and pre-death or deathbed visions.

Having this conversation about dying did at least open Mom up to talking about the fact that she wanted a simple Mass when she died and that she wanted the Mass at St. Giles in Oak Park where she and Dad had been parishioners since 1957. She didn't want all the music we had for Dad's Mass because music wasn't important to her the way it had been to Dad, and she wanted the money from her small insurance policy to be used for a nice memorial luncheon afterwards. I already knew that, like Dad, Mom wanted to be cremated, and I tucked all this information away in my memory for the future so I would be sure to carry out her wishes.

Several months after our conversation about the book <u>Home with God</u> Olga made her transition. Mom missed the relationship with her best friend very much and went deeper into depression. By the fall of 2007 Mom had retreated further into her own world, sleeping more during the day, reporting troubling dreams, no longer participating in the activities where she lived, and not eating well. She would eat the breakfast her caregiver made her, but then would not eat much when she went down for lunch or dinner. In fact, her tablemates reported to the nurse that they were worried that Mom was only eating a couple bites of dessert at dinner and nothing else. This was reported to the Executive Director of the facility who had the nurse weigh Mom. Indeed, she had lost five pounds in two months so they were concerned about her wellbeing.

Mom reported the dreams she had been having were quite disturbing. Appearing confused, she said, "In my dreams I got myself in a real mess with (members of her family of origin or with friends). I was so glad when I woke up and knew the dreams weren't real. But, I'm so confused when I wake up. I don't know if it's day or night, what day it is, or where I am."

In trying to normalize her experience, I replied, "Mom, it's not unusual after a deep dream experience to have it take time to feel like yourself again and come back to reality." I didn't say anything to Mom, but I noticed that all the people in the dreams she told me about had already died. It made me wonder if she was meeting them on the astral and trying to resolve situations she'd created for herself earlier in her life. Perhaps the confusion when she woke up was because her soul was traveling outside of her physical body. Was it possible that Mom was starting to experience her life review, somehow knowing on a subconscious level that her death was approaching? I did not discuss these possibilities with Mom because I knew the ideas were not part of her paradigm. I began to wonder if her withdrawal was due to the depression and/or if she were in the beginning stages of her dying process. It was all difficult to differentiate though I was hyper vigilant about listening to Mom's language for clues as to what was going on with her.

Mom experienced a big blow to her wellbeing in November 2007 when it was brought to my attention that the corporation that owns the facility Mom lived in had made a decision that if the people in the independent living facility (where Mom was) who had Life Care Contracts chose to spend their savings down paying for care-givers rather than go over to the assisted living section of the nursing home, their Life Care Contract would be canceled and made null and void. We had hired part time caregivers to help Mom for the past two years. Without them Mom's only recourse was the nursing home. I had an attorney look at the corporation's notification letter and the original contract Mom and Dad signed in 1998 and he felt that we had to follow through with the move to the nursing home facility.

Not knowing how long Mom might live (her father died at 98 years old and one of her brothers died a month before he turned 100) we couldn't risk losing the security of the Life Care Contract. When I broke the news to Mom she took it very hard. Even though she was evaluated and assigned to the assisted living floor of the nursing home where interference in her life would be minimal, to her the nursing home was a death sentence. After all, it was where Dad and all her friends from the independent living facility, including Olga, had gone to die. My siblings and I tried to play up all the positive aspects of the move, but it was clear she wasn't fully convinced.

Once the decision to move had been made I had three weeks to downsize Mom to a smaller one-bedroom apartment on the assisted living floor (first floor) of the nursing home. This meant sorting through her belongings, packing up, giving away, donating, figuring out a floor plan for the furniture that she would take to the new living space, moving everything, unpacking, etc. I took great care in clearing negative energy from the new apartment and bringing in positive loving energy that was calm and welcoming.

In the late afternoon on Monday, December 2, 2007 my sister and I brought Mom over to her new apartment. As we entered the building my sister noted that Mass was being said in the large room on the first floor, and we said it must be a good sign, a blessing that we could all receive Communion together on Mom's first day in her new home. The three of us went in to receive Communion before we took Mom to see her new apartment. Upon entering the apartment she had tears in her eyes and said, "I never thought it would look so beautiful." And so a new chapter of caring for Mom began.

CHAPTER 3

A New Home but the Same Self

For the first couple of months in the new apartment Mom seemed to be making a good adjustment. The Activities Director was successful in getting her to participate in some activities, she was eating better, and because she was always given her medications on schedule, there were no setbacks like she had had when she was living independently and forgot to take her medications. We had hoped that with more attention at the nursing home Mom's interest in life might perk up. However, the newness wore off and within four to five weeks Mom seemed to sink even deeper into the depression. A psychiatrist was called in to do an evaluation. He changed her antidepressant in hopes that the switch would be more stimulating for her brain and would help her feel more energetic, but it didn't seem to work. Mom was again sleeping the day away, and she asked me to call her to be sure she was up for lunch and dinner every day. In addition, she started having troubling dreams again and was also reporting more physical pain and discomfort. One of the issues with depression in the senior population, which often goes undiagnosed, is that when one is depressed and in the throes of anxiety and dark or fearful thoughts and feelings, the person may feel disconnected from God and/or their spiritual resources.

I encouraged Mom to say the Rosary to distract herself from her emotional and physical pain, but she said she kept forgetting the prayers recited with the Rosary and was no longer able to contemplate on its mysteries. She remembered the Our Father (Lord's Prayer) and the Glory Be but couldn't remember all of the Apostles' Creed or the Hail Mary, so she gave up on saying the Rosary. The Rosary has been a major influence in Roman Catholic thought for over 500 years, and it is the essence of Catholic devotion in which vocal and mental prayers unite the whole person in meditation on the central mysteries of Christian belief. The Rosary thus joins the human race to God through Mary whom God chose to be Christ's mother and intercessor for the human race.

My attempts at helping Mom learn to alleviate the physical, psychological and emotional pain by using prayers, breathing techniques, guided imagery or visualizations were met with strong resistance on her part. I'm sure part of her resistance had to do with her depression. In despair, she'd say, "Julie, I just can't do it. I can't seem to pray anymore. And the guided imagery CDs you brought over are not for me. I never could use my imagination or tell stories like your dad did." In light of her difficulties with these things I resolved that if she couldn't pray for herself, I would certainly continue praying for her and sending her healing light and love.

On numerous occasions I heard Mom say, "I offer up my pain and suffering for the poor souls in purgatory." It was a phrase I hadn't heard since Catholic grammar school. The Catechism of the Catholic Church defines purgatory as a "purification, so as to achieve the holiness necessary to enter the joy of heaven," which is experienced by those "who die in God's grace and friendship, but still imperfectly purified." The purification is necessary because, as Scripture teaches, nothing unclean will enter the presence of God in heaven

(Rev. 21:27). [1] Personally, I don't believe that God punishes us. I believe we are each created out of pure love and that our divine birthright is to be healthy, whole, happy and joyful. My experience is that we humans punish our selves and each other.

Thinking back to our conversation about the <u>Home with God</u> book I wondered if Mom thought she needed to go to purgatory after she died in order to be punished or to be purged of sins or offenses before she could go to heaven. Was the fear that Mom had about not being forgiven and not being worthy of going into the Light or going to Heaven lowering her energetic vibration? I wondered what affect her depression was having on her vibrational energy compared to what her energy would be like if she were peaceful, calm, and happy.

Why is vibration important in the dying process? In an excerpt from a workshop in North Los Angeles, California on August 18, 2002 Abraham stated:

> We are all Vibrational Beings. You're like a receiving mechanism that when you set your tuner to the station, you're going to hear what's playing. Whatever you are focused upon is the way you set your tuner, and when you focus there for as little as 17 seconds, you activate that vibration within you. Once you activate a vibration within you, Law of Attraction begins responding to that vibration, and you're off and running—whether it's something wanted or unwanted. (Abraham-Hicks.com)

In other words, the vibrational content of thoughts, words, and emotions determines what you are attracting and creating in your life. Jim Self in his e-book <u>The Shift</u>[2] states that

---
[1] Retrieved 11.04.08 from www.catholic.com/library/purgatory.asp
[2] www.masteringalchemy.com

thoughts are electrical and emotions are magnetic. They can work positively or negatively for you in aligning your personal vibrational frequency.

For example if one has negative thoughts (electrical) such as "I am not worthy of love" and consciously or unconsciously fears (magnetic) not being in a healthy, loving relationship with God or others, that person may attract negative emotions such as anxiety, despair, depression or physical discomfort to them self not to mention an unhealthy relationship. Mom was experiencing all of these states of being—anxiety, depression, despair, and physical pain. In contrast, if one is experiencing positive thoughts and is resonating with the higher vibrations of love, joy, or peace then a more positive state of physical well-being will be experienced and positive people will be attracted to that person.

Not judging Mom's belief about purgatory, I thought about my personal belief, which is that for each of us, our higher self or soul is complete and perfect in the eyes of God. It is our rational and subconscious minds that limit our thoughts and beliefs about who we really are, who our true selves are. Those limiting beliefs are based on messages we have absorbed from our environment, education, families of origin, culture, religion, society, politics, etc.

Since Mom was struggling with depression, troubling dreams, physical pain, and seemed to be fearful about going to purgatory, I was concerned that she was creating a negative vibration around herself and I didn't want her to attract even more discomfort.

In hopes of raising her vibration, I checked in psychically with Mom's higher self for permission and made a deliberate decision that each time I was with her I would discuss happier, more fun-filled, and joyful memories about the past. To this end I shared happy recollections from my childhood, memories of her doing nice things for people, and talked about what an amazing needlework artist and wonderful grandmother she was. I asked her to tell me about the happiest memories from her childhood, being a mom, and the many years of teaching needlework. I was attempting to shift her negative self-limiting beliefs to help her raise her vibrational level and hopefully help her heal emotionally, psychologically, and spiritually. It was also a way to assist Mom with her life review process. Sharing stories and memories did make her smile and laugh during the time I was with her, which was encouraging. I would also give her healing Reiki to help move energy and improve her mood. However, none of it seemed to have a lasting effect.

During the first week of April 2008 I was visiting Mom and we were in her bedroom talking. She was sitting on the side of her bed looking down at the floor, her shoulders drooped and her back was bent over as if she could no longer carry her own weight. She stated very matter-of-factly, "I can't do it anymore."

I sat down next to her on the bed, my mind racing, "What do you mean Mom? What is it? Are you talking about life?"

In a very woeful voice she said, "No, not life. It's just too much effort to get up every morning and have to sponge bathe myself and get myself dressed. I don't have the energy to do it anymore." Both of these tasks were requirements to live on the assisted living floor.

I took her hand in mine, looked her in the eyes and said, "Mom, just say the word and I'll get the ball rolling to move you upstairs to a floor where you will get more help."

Trying to sit up a little taller she said, "I can't do that to you. You just moved me in here a few months ago." I felt so sad for the inner struggle she was having and the effort it took her to make it through each day and I could sense what a crushing blow it would be for her to move from the assisted living floor to a regular nursing home floor. "Mom, that doesn't matter. I'm happy to move you upstairs if it will help you feel better and give you more comfort and peace of mind."

Her final response was, "We'll see. I don't know if I'm ready to give up this apartment."

CHAPTER 4

Falling Down and Moving Up

The week after I had the talk with Mom about moving upstairs, I went to Worcester, Massachusetts for five days, April 8-12th, to attend a conference on Integrating Mindfulness-Based Interventions into Medicine, Health Care, and the Larger Society. In between sessions on Thursday, April 10th, I checked my phone messages and found out that Mom had fallen in her bathroom earlier in the day. Fortunately, the nurse's aid was there at the time so Mom received immediate medical attention. She was taken to the nearby hospital where it was determined that she fractured her right hip. My sister who worked at the hospital where Mom was taken had been notified about the accident and was able to meet Mom in the emergency room. My brother flew in from California on Friday and was there to greet her in her room when she got out of recovery after the hip surgery. I arrived home late Saturday evening and went to see Mom the first time on Sunday. She was heavily sedated and could not eat, so she was receiving IV fluids. She was also receiving a unit of blood, as she was anemic after the surgery. The surgery and sedation left her so weak it was difficult to understand anything she said, and I stayed with her most of the day trying to provide as much comfort as possible.

To my surprise when I got to the hospital early the next morning, they were already preparing to discharge Mom. I was shocked they were going to send home a 92 year-old woman who was only three days post surgery and very weak, as she essentially hadn't eaten anything for five days. As the holder of her power of attorney, I had to assertively advocate with the orthopedic resident for Mom to be allowed to stay one more day to regain some strength and to better manage her pain before making the transfer back to the nursing home.

Naturally, the next day when we did transfer Mom back to the nursing home, there was no way she could go back to her apartment on the assisted living floor. She was given a Medicare room on the 4th floor, a medical floor. After Mom got settled in the room, she asked where she was. It was normal that she might be confused since she had such limited vision and the space was not familiar to her.

I said, "Mom you're at the (I named the nursing home) on the 4th floor. You're apartment is downstairs here on the first floor."

Her reply shook me. "You mean it took all that to get up here?"

My heart was breaking and my throat tightened as I tried to hold back the tears. "Oh Mom, it didn't have to take all that to get up here. You could have just asked."

"No," she said, "it had to take all that." Mom was a Taurus, very stubborn at times. She had to do things her way. I was filled with sadness about the difficult path she had chosen to get herself upstairs.

Had Mom on some unconscious level attracted the injury to herself? Why couldn't she accept my offer less than two weeks previously that I'd be happy to move her upstairs? Was it important that she fall while I was away? In her book, <u>We Live Forever: The Real Truth About Death,</u> P.M.H. Atwater writes, "A human being not in proper balance physically, emotionally, mentally, and spiritually will subconsciously set up a vibrational signal which will attract to him or her the very diseases, accident, or incidents necessary for that individual's redirection, rebirth, or death." It was important for me to trust that there was a divine reason for all that happened and that both Mom and I had some important lessons to learn and some healing to do.

We were all concerned that the hip fracture might add to Mom's depression and reduce the quality of her life. The dangers of hip fractures for the elderly are reported over and over in the media. One in four elderly people that break a hip die within a year,[3] and this made me wonder how this would all play out for Mom.

During the first two weeks on the 4th floor it was apparent that Mom didn't have the same "I'll get over this and be back home soon" attitude that she had shown after her other hospitalizations. She was not eating or drinking much, was loosing weight, and she chose to participate only minimally in her physical therapy. Of course part of this was due to pain—chronic back pain, pain from the hip surgery and having a pin placed in her right leg with screws at the top and bottom to anchor it, and from a very deep bed sore on her tailbone that she got during her four day stay in the hospital. Trying to keep her comfortable so she would have a positive attitude was challenging.

Mom had been diagnosed with first stage Alzheimer's disease in April 2006. Her cognitive abilities, except for her some short-term memory problems, were stable until the accident. She could carry on wonderful conversations, ask about the kids, answer questions about the past, do math calculations

---

[3] Retrieved 11.04.08 from www.usatoday.com/news/health/2001-05-03-hips.htm

in her head, had an accurate sense of her financial situation, and more. However, after the surgery we all noticed a very rapid decline in Mom's cognitive abilities, both her short and long-term memories. For example, she couldn't grasp the idea of using the call button and so might lie in a soiled diaper or be experiencing severe pain for a couple of hours before someone came to check on her. Wondering if the sudden cognitive decline could be from Mom's surgery, I read some research articles that provided evidence that elderly people (those over 65 years old) have a higher risk of cognitive dysfunction (cognitive speed, speed of general information processing, and memory loss) after surgery performed under general anesthesia.

Even though the nursing home Mom was in is one of the best in the Chicago area, with more staff per patient on the medical floor, situations arose that gave me pause about the quality of Mom's care. I felt strongly that someone needed to be at the nursing home for at least a little while every day to be with Mom and to advocate for her care. With her extremely poor vision, full-blown Alzheimer's disease, and broken hip, Mom's care was a challenge without someone who could be with her around the clock. Mom didn't have the financial resources for that level of care. My sister had struggled with depression and wisely knew her limits. She felt she could only visit Mom on Saturday, so that meant I needed to be there six days a week.

It is important for each of us to know our personal limitations—emotional and physical health, energy, time, and finances in regards to the frequency of our visits to friends and loved ones so the time we spend with them is in the higher vibrational frequencies of love, harmony, forgiveness, and peace. I promised myself that I would take care of my physical and emotional health during this process so I could make Mom my priority. I made the decision to maintain only current clients in my private therapy practice of transpersonal and health psychology and facilitate the Personal Transformation Intensive® weekends that I was committed to, but I would refer out anyone new who called to see about starting therapy with me. It was important to me that I keep my vibrational level high, to be with Mom in love, and to not go into a place of resentment or anger because I was too tired or overworked.

Because I had a plan for my own health and wellbeing I was able to enjoy spending time with Mom. As a result of the Alzheimer's disease our conversations became more limited, but holding her hand, massaging her shoulders and the back of her neck, and putting lotion on her hands became part of our daily routine. It was obvious she enjoyed the touching and the nurturing. Due to her weight loss, Mom's clothes were very loose on her. This was unsettling as Mom had always dressed beautifully and was meticulous about her appearance. To help raise her spirits, I ordered five new blouses, two new sweaters, and two pairs of slacks for her 93rd birthday that was fast approaching. I hoped that some new clothes would bring her joy, and when the clothes arrived and she wore them, the nurses and nurse's aides commented daily about how beautiful she looked. She'd smile and soak in the compliments.

Mom's 93rd birthday was May 9th. I intuitively knew it would be her last birthday and wanted to make it special. I ordered a cake big enough for all the residents and staff on the floor, brought in pretty napkins, plates, colorful Mylar Happy Birthday balloons, and flowers. Mom could no longer use the phone because of her poor vision and Alzheimer's disease, and I knew people wouldn't call her. So I dialed family members and a couple of her friends and held my cell phone up to her ear so she could hear birthday greetings from loved ones. It was a special day.

I was glad we had the special birthday celebration for Mom when we did because five days later she contracted a virulent, highly contagious flu virus that swept through the 4th floor affecting many of the patients and staff. The dehydration Mom experienced not only weakened her physically, it also caused her cognitive abilities to decline even further. There was a 24-hour period where I called my siblings and said to be on alert, as I didn't think Mom was going to make it. I kept vigil by her bed, moistening her lips and trying to get small amounts of water in her mouth with a spoon. Between not eating well and the flu Mom's weight dwindled to 94 pounds. When she was admitted to the 4th floor after the fall, she had weighed 107 pounds so it was a significant weight loss. Before Mom got the flu the Director of Nursing on the floor told me that May 21st would be Mom's last day of Medicare coverage and she would have to move to another private room on the same floor. So in addition to coping with her serious illness I had to get everything out of her apartment on the first floor and close it down.

When I found out that Mom would be terminated from Medicare coverage, I requested that she have an evaluation by the same hospice organization that had done such a wonderful job of caring for my father the last seven months of his life. While many people think hospice care is for the last few weeks or days of life this couldn't be further from the truth. Our experience with both parents was that when the diagnosis was made that they would not be getting any better physically, the hospice and palliative care organization offered higher quality and more compassionate care, tailored more specifically to my parents' needs and wishes, than the nursing home had been able to provide them.

Mom easily qualified for hospice and interestingly had the same diagnosis that Dad had, "failure to thrive." Mom had an interdisciplinary hospice team consisting of a registered nurse, a licensed clinical social worker, hospice physician, certified nurse's aide, music therapist, chaplain, and a hospice-trained volunteer, which greatly improved the quality of her life. They worked cooperatively with the nursing home staff and provided holistic care, managed her pain and symptoms, and helped me advocate for a higher quality of care for her. They were all tuned in to Mom's physical, emotional, psychological, and spiritual needs, and their visits provided her more socialization and connection with people who cared about her than the staff at the nursing home was able to provide. One of my goals in bringing in hospice was that Mom wouldn't have as many hours spent alone where she had historically experienced fear, anxiety, despair and hopelessness—emotions of the lower vibrational levels. The hospice team brought Mom understanding, compassion, acceptance and love—all higher vibration emotions and life views. I will always be grateful to each of them for the love and support they gave to Mom, our family, and the nursing home staff.

Even with the hospice team in place, there was the need to constantly advocate for Mom's physical safety, as she wouldn't remember that she didn't have the strength in her right hip to stand or walk by herself, and sometimes she'd try to get out of her wheelchair. I also had to advocate for her by encouraging the staff to watch for signs of anxiety, pain, and urinary tract infections and give her the appropriate medications when needed. Even so, I'd often pick up on these symptoms before the staff would. This meant constant communication with both the nursing home staff and the hospice team as well as attending regular staff meetings about Mom's care plan.

To me, quality of care also meant doing things to lift her spirits, so I'd routinely rub lotion in her hands and arms and give her mini-facials and manicures. Touch is so important to the well being of the elderly, and mom was no exception. She soaked it all in just like the lotions soaked into her thinning, fragile skin. I also brought a CD player for her room and always saw to it that gentle, soothing music was playing when I left. Two of my major goals in Mom's care were to create a situation where she experienced the best quality of life she could have given her limitations and to be sure that she was safe in every aspect of her whole being.

Several times during the four months that they cared for Mom the hospice staff asked me, "Are you aware how much your mother trusts you? You have made a difference in her life." I considered it an honor to be able to care for and nurture Mom. I knew that it was part of our karma that during these last months of her life I was to nurture her—something she didn't know as a child or in her marriage, and something she often said she didn't know how to do as a mother. Several times when I was growing up I heard her say, "I don't know how to parent because my mother died when I was 13 years and I was raised by a much older father and five older brothers." Mom saw herself as handicapped and a victim her whole life. She was born with a massive port-wine birthmark that covered a large area on the right side of her face and as a child she often felt rejected by peers because of her appearance. I wanted her to leave this physical life feeling cherished and knowing what it's like to be nurtured and loved so she'd be empowered to love herself and others more in her next life, if she chose to be reincarnated.

The cognitive decline that Mom experienced after the surgery and flu left her with very little short-term memory and no long-term memory. She would often start a sentence and forget what she wanted to say. She wouldn't remember that someone had just been there to visit her ten minutes before I arrived or she wouldn't remember if she'd eaten breakfast, let alone what she had eaten. She couldn't track a very long conversation, so I kept them short and positive. I continued telling her about happy memories or funny stories from our past together. Her memories of the past were completely gone. She'd ask about her father or her siblings, all of whom had died many years ago.

Interestingly, her dreams stopped completely. When I asked if she had any dreams about friends or family she replied "No. I'm glad that's not coming forward any more." I found her statement to be interesting and insightful considering the fact that she had no apparent memory of her past.

When Mom would ask about the past, I'd take the opportunity to paint a visual picture of what going to heaven might be like. In one of our conversations she asked very sincerely, "How's Bill?"

"Do you mean Uncle Bill, Mom?"

"Yes."

Reaching over and holding her hand I replied, "Well Mom, I think he's doing just fine. This is 2008 and Uncle Bill died in 1987. He is having a wonderful time up in heaven. He's looking down at us with a big smile and saying we'll have a wonderful celebration when you get here. He's waiting. He'll be there to help you cross into the Light when you are ready."

She smiled, almost laughed and said, "Julie, you say the funniest things sometimes. What did Bill die from? Was it his heart?" Then, it was my turn to smile. I would go on to answer all her questions about the particulars. Not knowing what Mom was absorbing spiritually or cognitively, I took advantage of each of these golden (lost memory) opportunities to see if I could help Mom create a different picture of where she might go when she died. In <u>Home with God</u> Neale Donald Walsch states, "God will allow you to create in the moment of your death whatever experience you wish."

Another cognitive aspect about Mom that had changed was that she was much calmer, sweeter, and kinder. She was expressing all those sentiments I longed to hear from her as a child. My heart was healing and opening more and more to her. There was also a child-like quality about her that was lovable. I found myself imagining what she was like as a child, and I felt incredible compassion for her difficult, painful childhood. We all commented about her smiles as she had such a sweet smile and we had never seen her smile so much in her life. This time with Mom was very healing for me and soon I was aware that the hurts I had been holding on to for so many years were no longer there. The tenderness and love I felt for Mom are hard to express in words. I told her every day how much I loved her, and I thanked her for being my mother and my children's grandmother. I am sure that all the personal growth work and spiritual work I have done helped to lay the groundwork for this healing.

After lunch or dinner I would take Mom for a stroll in her wheelchair and then get her ready for a nap or for bed, depending on the time of day. She would often ask me to stay until she fell asleep so it just became routine for me to stay. I would sit in a chair that was positioned several feet away from the foot of her bed and send her Reiki energy while silently asking that her Higher Self or soul place the Reiki energy exactly where it needed to be and use it for her higher good. Reiki is a Universal Life Force healing energy that is safe and pure and enhances the body's natural ability to heal itself physically, emotionally, psychologically, and spiritually. As such, there was the possibility that the Reiki may have assisted in reducing Mom's chronic back pain and increasing her feelings of wellbeing. I always asked Mom's soul for guidance because only the soul knows the highest good of the individual and that good must take priority over physical healing. In other words, the soul may have been directing the Reiki to help Mom heal on a spiritual level, not on a physical level.

In July when I'd sit and watch Mom falling asleep, I started noticing that her aura or Luminous Energy Field (an emanation of vital energy which radiates around natural objects, including human beings, animals and plants) was slowly drawing in closer and closer to her body. I took this as a sign that her life force energy was slowly leaving. I am a Reiki Phowa Practitioner so I thought it was time to do the Reiki Phowa for Mom. The Phowa is a centuries old Tibetan practice to help the dying prepare for a good death. It is a beautiful process invoking healing, forgiveness, and compassion and bringing in spiritual light that provides the person a deep sense of peace and serene detachment, so the soul is prepared to make it's journey into the Light. The practitioner sets the intention that from the point of doing the Reiki Phowa all the healing angels and divine guides or spiritual beings that have been invoked, such as Jesus, God, or Mother Mary, will remain until the moment of death when the person merges with the Light, or in the Tibetan belief, with the wisdom mind of the Buddha.

Doing the Reiki Phowa for Mom was beautiful but tearful, as I had visions of her filled with the violet, orange, and golden white lights ready to merge with God. The tearful part was the peacefulness I saw in Mom. I said prayers of gratitude that she was now experiencing calm and peace and not the fear and depression she'd struggled with previously. In addition, it gave me tremendous comfort to know that this Tibetan method of attaining enlightenment was already set in place in case I was not able to be with Mom at the time of her transition.

In July I began thinking that Mom was traveling on the astral plane to be with me when I was away from her. The astral plane in theosophical belief, esoteric philosophy and some religious teaching is a level of existence outside the physical human body where the spirit or soul goes between death and entry into the spirit world. It's also where the soul goes at night when we are dreaming. On several occasions I'd wake at night hearing Mom calling my name and sensing her presence. I would tell her she was all right, that she was safe, that I loved her and it was time for her to go back to sleep. I knew it worked because I would no longer hear her calling my name once I reassured her.

One morning I had to go out to Wheaton, IL to take care of some business for a workshop I was organizing. Later in the day when I arrived to visit Mom, she inquired, "What were you doing in DeKalb this morning?" I was surprised because I hadn't mentioned my plans to Mom at all. You may say Wheaton isn't DeKalb. Yes, that's true, but Wheaton is half way to DeKalb and I was on the same toll-way to Wheaton that I would take to DeKalb. Was it coincidence or was Mom traveling on the astral plane? Was she beginning to have out-of-body experiences in preparation for her death experience?

In thinking about Mom, I recalled a beautiful story Jean Houston, philosopher, author and scholar, told about her Sicilian grandmother's death. One hour before her grandmother died she woke up after having been in a coma and vegetative state for six years. When a relative commented about her being in a coma for so many years, her grandmother said, "Oh, but you wouldn't believe the places I've been." In regards to working with patients or family members in a coma or with dementia or Alzheimer's disease Dr. Houston cautions that we not think that because their surface mind is not focused and functioning in a normal way, that their depth mind is not traveling and preparing and joining a much larger universe.[4]

It would be hard to know whether Mom was traveling and joining the larger universe unless I could have asked her, but

---
[4] As seen in Experiencing the Soul, 2005, DVD

with the decline in her cognitive abilities, there were many questions left both unanswered and unasked. I was getting a stronger and stronger sense that Mom was not going to live until Christmas. I called my brother and sister before Patrick came in from California for a visit in August and explained that I'd really like us all to meet in Mom's room on Saturday and get a picture of the three of us siblings together with her. We normally didn't all visit Mom at the same time because it was too exhausting for her, but we were thrilled that the photos captured some of her last smiles. After Mom died, when I looked back at the photos from her 90th birthday celebration, I found there was not one picture of the three of us with Mom so I appreciated following my intuition and orchestrating the mini photo session on August 16th.

The week following Patrick's visit there was a new male patient sitting at Mom's lunch table. Mom said, "That's Dwight Follett."

I replied, "I can see why you think that Mom. He has the same shaped face and he's about the same size, but Mr. Follett died over twenty years ago."

With a very surprised look on her face she said, "I didn't know that."

I could understand Mom's confusion with her memory and her vision losses, but I was still wondering about her comment when I wheeled her away from the table that day. She pointed over to a corner and said, "Your dad's over there. Don't you want to go and say hi?" At the time I thought it was her low vision playing tricks on her, but later I wondered if Dad had come for a pre-death visit. I wish I had asked her if she and Dad had been conversing or if he had a message for her. I encourage you to listen carefully and be lovingly curious when comments such as those my mother and father made to me shortly before they transitioned are made by your loved ones or patients.

There were also some brief moments that Mom seemed very lucid, which was the case when Rich and I went to visit and feed her dinner on Labor Day. It was a beautiful evening so after dinner we wheeled her outside to the patio garden to get some fresh air. After commenting to her about the weather, the flowers, and the people passing, she piped up and pointed to a gate and announced, "I think we can get out over there."

Our reply was, "Shall we go see?"

Mom gave us an enthusiastic, "Yes!"

We were like three naughty kids sneaking out of the house and going some place we shouldn't. Not knowing we would actually be leaving the facility grounds we hadn't signed Mom out at the front desk of the nursing home. We were sure that there must be video cameras recording our get-away and that we'd be reprimanded when we got back! Even so, we opened the gate and took Mom for a ride in her wheelchair down to the corner, halfway down the next block and then finally headed back to the nursing home. She was smiling during the walk and we were commenting on the different sights, sounds, and smells. The little jaunt seemed to satisfy her curiosity. Little did we know that "I think we can get out over there." would turn out to be a metaphor or foreshadowing that Mom would soon be making her way out of this physical life and finding her way Home.

CHAPTER 5

Another Fall, One Last Move

The next day when I visited Mom I explained that I would be going to Wheaton the following day for a six-day training. I told her that this was the workshop I had been organizing since the prior January. Mom was familiar with my going away to facilitate personal growth workshops at a retreat center in Wheaton, so she seemed fine with it. I told her that both my sister and the nursing home staff had my cell phone number in case she needed me and that I would be thinking about her and sending her love every day.

The training was a pre-requisite for people who want to study and earn certification as Level II Breath Therapists, and interestingly the material on this level focused on birth and death issues. As promised, I checked my cell phone several times a day and all was well until the fourth day of the training. In the late afternoon, when I checked to see if I had any messages, I saw that the nursing home had tried to call. I immediately called back and was told that Mom had fallen and was taken to the emergency room with a suspected hip fracture. My heart sank. Not again! I was able to reach my sister at the hospital and learned that Mom was already in a room and Mary Anne was with her. Mary Anne confirmed that she had fractured her hip, the left one this time. She said

Mom was on pain medication, was resting comfortably, and the orthopedic team was thinking of doing surgery the next day, Sunday, or Monday.

My immediate reaction was that I should leave the training and go right to the hospital. As holder of Mom's Power of Attorney I felt I should be there to make any important medical decisions. I was feeling incredibly sad and the tears just flowed. Then I took some deep breaths to try to get clarity and realized that, at least for that day, I would stay at the training. My sister assured me that she could handle the situation until I finished the training and encouraged me to stay.

As it turned out staying was a good choice for me. The timing of our next process in the group was perfect. It was Holotropic Breathwork™. In short, as defined by the Association for Holotropic Breathwork™ International, "Holotropic Breathwork™ is a safe and simple way to trigger experiences of non-ordinary consciousness that open us to psychic depths and spiritual understanding."[5] My experience with the Holotropic Breathwork™ process helped me come to understand fully that this was the end of Mom's life. Through the breathwork I first allowed myself to feel overwhelming grief and sadness, and then I saw all her loved ones in heaven with huge smiles cheering her on to come Home and join them in the Light.

In closing the experience, we were each given a large sheet of paper with a circle on it and a box of crayons with the instructions that we were to draw the first thing that came to us, be it a vision, a sense, or words, and allow the energy from the breathwork session to flow through us to create a mandala, which is a circular image that reflects natural and universal shapes and represents our cosmic connection and wholeness. Creating the mandala provided an opportunity

---
[5] www.breathwork.com

to bring into physical reality the multidimensionality of the physical, emotional, psychological and spiritual nature of the breathwork experience.

Here is my mandala.

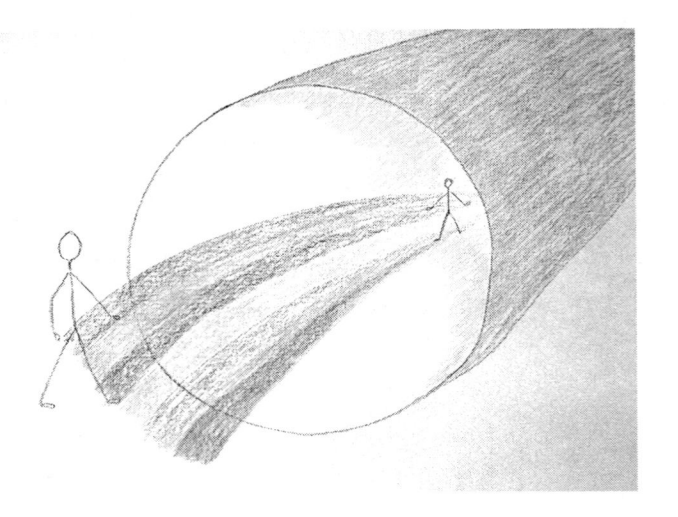

My mandala shows that I am there at the beginning of the rainbow bridge, encouraging Mom on her way and that she is in the channel, moving higher into the Light. The message that came to me was that I was to help Mom open all her chakras so Spirit could flow through her. I was to help her cross the rainbow bridge and go into the Light. I knew this message came from Divine Mother-Father God, that s/he would be there guiding me the whole way, and I cried tears of gratitude as I created my mandala.

Before going to the first class the next morning I called my sister to get a report on how Mom was doing. Mary Anne related the news that orthopedics could not do surgery that day because Mom's body had gone into shock from the fall. I learned that at the nursing home Mom had been left in her wheelchair at the lunch table and 10-15 minutes later a nurse's aide had come upstairs from her lunch break and found Mom in her room on the floor outside her bathroom. It's not known, or was never revealed to me, who took Mom to her room and left her there, or how long she had been lying on the floor before the aide found her. Her blood pressure was extremely elevated, she had a terrible urinary tract infection (E. coli) which she must have had for days before the fall, her blood was not clotting so she needed vitamin K, and her blood sugar levels were so high they had to give her insulin to bring her glucose levels down to normal. In spite of all these serious issues, orthopedics was planning to do the surgery Monday and Mary Anne had signed the release papers for the operation.

After hearing about Mom's physical condition I became very concerned about whether or not surgery was in Mom's best interest, and I took time to meditate about the situation prior to joining the training. In the meditation, I received the information that Mom should not have surgery until I had more information about her condition. Not knowing if Mom's hospice team had been notified by the nursing home or my sister after Mom's fall, I called and left a message for Mom's hospice nurse care coordinator and asked that the team go over to the hospital to evaluate the situation and get back to me. When the nurse care coordinator returned my call she said she and the team social worker would be at the hospital first thing in the morning to do an evaluation. I explained that I did not want Mom to have surgery until I could get to the hospital early Monday evening and have the hospice team's input. Though I was torn between going to the hospital and completing my commitment to this training, especially when it had taken me nine months to organize it, I knew Mom was in good hands with the hospice team.

That day I had another wonderful Holotropic Breathwork™ session, and I received several spiritual messages about being present with Mom during her dying process. I was to assist her in raising her vibration and help her know her Divine essence so she'd know she was worthy of merging with the Light. I was to release Mom with grace and ease, trust my inner knowing, and know my spiritual guides and angels would be with me during the process.

Again, after our sessions we all drew mandalas, and I let the drawing flow from my heart to create a mandala that incorporated the messages I had received. In this mandala I am the hands releasing Mom's beautiful, pure, bright essence to merge with the Light.

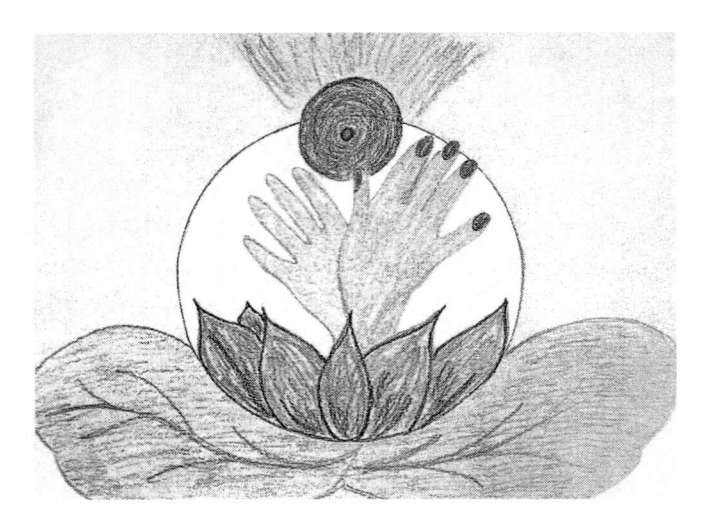

In Buddhism, the lotus flower with its roots in the mud, rising through the murky water to blossom clean and bright, symbolizes purity, resurrection and the enlightened being that emerges undefiled from the chaos and illusion of the world. In Tibetan Buddhism the most common prayer or mantra found everywhere is *Om Mani Padma Hum*. The translation is, "Hail to the jewel in the lotus." Spiritual teachers tell us that the blue pearl is the seed of consciousness; that it exists in each of us, and is the source from which our consciousness flows. It is sometimes called the "essence," the "body of the self," the "spark of God," and has been described as that which links our higher soul with the embodied soul. As with other messages I'd received during meditation, I was to help Mom's soul go into the Light.

Early Monday morning, September 8th, Mom's hospice team (doctor, nurse, and social worker) went to the hospital and did a thorough evaluation of her condition. Mom was still on the schedule for surgery and they had to work quickly to get her off the schedule. They informed the hospital staff that the signed surgical release was not valid as my sister did not hold Power of Attorney (POA) for Mom, and they presented a copy of the POA papers faxed from the nursing home showing I had POA. They explained that I wanted to cancel surgery until I knew what was in Mom's best interest. I was on the phone with the hospice nurse on and off all morning and I scheduled a meeting with hospice for 9:00 am Tuesday in Mom's room. When I called my sister and brother to let them know I had canceled the surgery they were fine with my decision. My sister said that the past two days of being with Mom had been a gift from me, as it had provided an opportunity for her to connect and have some much needed closure with her.

Our breathwork experience on Monday was a past-life regression session. I regressed to being a girl about 17-18 years old living in an Essene community around the time of Christ. I had traveled to a couple of different Essene communities to be trained by the elders and had gone through several spiritual initiations. As I had grown older I'd continued to receive initiations in the Essene Mystery Schools. The message of the session was that I already had the knowledge from the mystery schools to help Mom transition and I needed to be open to remembering it.

On Monday afternoon, as soon as the training was complete, I left for the hospital. When I got to Mom's room I gave her a kiss and told her I was there and that I loved her, but she didn't respond. I saw that she had taken off one of the leads to the monitor, as well as the blood oxygen level monitor that had been clipped to the end of one of her fingers. Even though an alarm was going off no one had come to the room to check on her. Mom was twisting the covers, one of her physical signs of agitation, and she seemed very confused. She didn't know who I was, and when I tried to take the lead out of her hand, she pushed my hand away. I suspected that she was struggling with delirium similar to what she had experienced several months before when she had suffered another bad urinary tract infection. I pressed the call button and asked for her nurse to come in. While waiting for the nurse to come, I tried to swab Mom's lips with a small sponge on a stick that was moistened with water. She shut her lips tightly, not allowing me to give her any moisture. When the nurse finally came, ten minutes after I called, I explained who I was and asked her to give Mom some Ativan, which was the medication she was being given for anxiety and agitation. The nurse brought the Ativan, gave it to Mom through her IV, put the leads back on her and reset the monitoring machine. The lack of response to the monitor alarms going off and the fact that I had to request medication for her made me question the quality of care Mom was getting at this hospital. The nurse told me Mom had refused her oral medications for the past two days. I wondered if these behaviors were a sign of delirium or if Mom was letting us know that she wanted to die. Was this her way of communicating her intention?

The nurse paged the orthopedic resident to come talk to me about surgery. He came to the room, introduced himself and said, "I understand you have questions about the surgery."

Looking him straight in the eye and with my most erect posture, I said, "No. I don't know if there will be surgery."

He told me that the fracture in the left hip was just like the fracture that Mom had experienced in April and that they would put in a pin with screws at the top and bottom to stabilize it. He said that once the surgery was done and the fracture was set Mom would have less pain. After I heard him out I explained that Mom was a hospice patient, that I needed to meet with her team the next morning to discuss what was most compassionate for her considering her physical, emotional, and psychological state of being, and that I'd let him know my decision after that meeting had taken place.

After my meeting with the surgeon I spent a few more hours with Mom before I kissed her good bye and told her I'd be back in the morning. I left her resting peacefully after her pain and anti-anxiety medication had taken effect.

The next day I drove to the hospital for my 9:00 am meeting with Mom's hospice team. As I pulled into the parking lot at the hospital around 8:45 am my cell phone rang. I saw it was a blocked call, probably one of the hospice team members. When I answered it, the nurse on the line asked in a very concerned voice, "Julie, how are you?"

"I just pulled into the parking lot at the hospital," I replied.

"I'm so sorry to hear about Mary," she said.

Not understanding, I asked, "What are you talking about?"

"We just got a text message saying that your mother passed away. We're so surprised. I'm so sorry."

That can't be, I thought to myself. The hospital would call me first, wouldn't they? My heart was racing. "But, no one called me. I have to get off the phone and go inside and see what the situation is," I said. " Will you please still come to the hospital?"

I'm sure she must have heard the confusion and sense of urgency in my voice. "Yes, we'll be there as soon as possible," she responded.

As I got out of the car and headed into the hospital the adrenalin was rushing through my system, my heart was pounding and racing so fast I thought it was going to burst out of my chest, and the tears were starting to flow. I couldn't believe it. *Mom, I thought we had a deal.* I was aware that I didn't know what the *deal* was, but it couldn't be true that Mom was dead. The messages in the breath therapy sessions were about me being present to help Mom go into the Light. Did her soul have a different agenda? It didn't make sense to me. Time seemed to slow down and it felt like it took me forever to walk to the right elevator and for the doors to open. People were staring at me as the tears rolled down my cheeks. I got to Mom's floor, walked in the room, and SHE WAS ALIVE! I literally had to stop and take several deep breaths to try to calm myself and restore my balance. I kissed Mom's forehead and let her know I was there and how much I loved her, but she was unresponsive. She had already slipped into a semi-conscious state that she would remain in until she died. From this point on we had no two-way verbal communication, something I was missing already in addition to missing looking into her eyes.

I went in the bathroom to wash my face and soon one of the hospice physicians that had been seeing Mom since May arrived. We sat down to talk about Mom's condition and discuss the options. The first was surgery that could be very painful and speed up her demise, if she even made it through the procedure. He said even with surgery Mom would never be physically or mentally where she was prior to this recent fall. I knew the toll the general anesthesia from right hip surgery in April had taken on her cognition, and I couldn't imagine what another surgery might do. The other option was to refuse surgery and see how Mom did, though without surgery her mobility would be extremely limited since the hip would not be stabilized. The hospice nurse and social worker arrived while we were talking, and the physician said he'd step out into the hall and leave the three of us to talk.

My body was still physically shaking with the after effects of the rush of adrenalin from when I had heard Mom had died, and I was still very teary, even more so thinking about the need to make the decision about surgery. Both hospice staff members apologized profusely about the mistake and said that someone at the office in entering a "change of status" on Mom had incorrectly checked the death box. Who would have thought something so small as a little check box could cause such so much emotional upheaval?

Mom had signed a Living Will so I knew she didn't want to be on life support. She had also verbalized prior to her first hip fracture that living was an incredible struggle for her. The first fracture and ensuing Alzheimer's disease had even further decreased her quality of life. These were things I had to take into consideration when making a decision about her surgery, and indeed her future care. I didn't know one could have so many thoughts go through their head in such a short period of time as I did. The hospice nurse went out to talk with the physician and came back to say that after evaluating Mom, reading the chart, and thinking about her whole being over the past four months that he had been caring for her, he felt her body had suffered so much shock from the fall that she probably would only live about another two weeks. If Mom didn't have surgery, the options were to keep her as a hospice patient at the hospital, move her back to the nursing home and stay under hospice care, or to move her to the hospice's In-Patient Unit (IPU) located in a nearby hospital.

I had to make a decision. I was crying, my heart was still racing and I was still feeling shaky and in shock from the incorrect news of Mom's passing. Choosing hospice over surgery also meant discontinuing everything by mouth, no IVs, and only medication to manage her pain, anxiety, and symptoms that would occur as her body became more dehydrated. In addition, in her current semi-conscious state, it was not safe to give her anything by mouth as she might not swallow correctly and there was danger of aspiration. Mom had been refusing her oral medications and food the past two days, so I felt she had already made a statement about her wishes by ceasing to eat and drink. I thoughtfully weighed all the options, connected with my heart, and asked God to help me make the right decision. In the end I consciously and lovingly chose for her not to have the surgery. And because I didn't feel she would get the quality of care she deserved at either the nursing home or the hospital I chose to have her transferred that afternoon to the hospice's In-patient Unit (IPU).

After I made the decision not to go through with the surgery and to have her moved I asked God for a sign that it was the right choice. The sign came when Mom, in a moment of pain, started saying the "Hail Mary". When we had prayed together over the past nine months, she didn't remember the whole prayer, but in that moment she said the entire "Hail Mary." I knew this was Mom's gift to me, a sign from God and Mom that the decision was what she wanted and was what was for her highest good. For those who aren't familiar with the prayer, it is:

> Hail Mary, full of grace,
> the Lord is with thee.
> Blessed art thou among women, and
> Blessed is the fruit of thy womb, Jesus.
> Holy Mary, Mother of God,
> Pray for us sinners now,
> and at the hour of death.
> Amen.

The prayer made me wonder if Mom was aware she was dying and praying for the help of the Christ's mother to protect her and intercede for her to go to heaven at the hour of her death.

As we were waiting for the private ambulance to come transfer Mom the priest from hospice that had been making weekly visits to Mom came by to see her. I felt it was important to honor Mom's Catholic traditions, so when he had first started seeing her I requested that he give her the Anointing of the Sick Sacrament, which is the Sacrament of God's strength, healing and forgiveness. I asked if he would please give Mom the Anointing of the Sick Sacrament again since she was now at a different phase of the dying process, and I told him the hospice physician said Mom probably had only two weeks to live. He agreed that he would try to come by IPU during the next couple of days.

CHAPTER 6

Creating and Holding a Sacred Space for Mom to Transition

Mom was transferred by ambulance to the hospice's In-Patient Unit at the nearby hospital by two paramedics who were very caring and kind, and I found the staff at IPU to be loving, gentle, and compassionate. Once she was settled I stayed for two shifts so the nurses and I could work together to observe Mom's pain and/or anxiety symptoms and see that she received Dilaudid for pain via a subcutaneous shunt and an oral Ativan called Intensol that is absorbed by the mucosa of the mouth, as needed. The staff lovingly repositioned Mom every four hours to prevent skin breakdown. They carefully timed her pain medication to help prevent discomfort when it was time to reposition her and because the left hip had to remain in a stable position Mom was always kept somewhat on her back. All in all I felt reassured that moving Mom to the IPU was the right decision; Mom would get the care she deserved.

However, I didn't feel comfortable with the energy in Mom's room. It felt cold and chaotic, so I planned to start working the next day to change the situation. I wanted Mom to be in the energy of love, peace and compassion, feeling safe, calm and tranquil as she had a lot of hard inner work to do physically, emotionally, psychologically and spiritually to prepare to depart this physical world.

My husband stopped by around dinnertime and brought something to eat as he had class that evening. He sat on the day bed in Mom's room, unwrapped a sandwich, took one bite and started chewing. The sound of the chewing in the quiet of the room was deafening, and he immediately sensed that it was not appropriate. Mom couldn't take anything by mouth so out of respect for her he chose to leave the room to finish eating. Before I went home that evening I said an invocation or prayer that I had often mentally said in the evenings before I kissed Mom good night in the nursing home:

> Divine Mother-Father God, Infinite Love and Wisdom, and all the angels and archangels, I invoke your divine healing, love, protection, and presence to be with Mom on all levels of her being - physically, mentally, emotionally, and spiritually—past, present, future and parallel lives as she lays down to rest. Place your shield of protection in and around Mom and protect her from all negative energy as she sleeps. May only healing transforming energy flow through her and around her at all times. So be it now. Blessed be. And so it is.

Tuesday night when I got home, and again before I left to visit Mom Wednesday morning, I sent emails to our relatives, Mom's friends, people in my spiritual community, my Master Mind groups, the nuns at the retreat center in Wheaton, anyone with whom Mom or I had a close connection. I called her friends all across the United States that didn't have email. I explained Mom's situation and said I would love as many people as possible praying for Mom to have a beautiful, peaceful transition. I knew the power of collectively holding the image of

Mom having a peaceful transition was very important. In <u>The Book of Kin</u> from The Ringing Cedar Series, Anastasia says:

> An image is an entity of energy created by human thought. It can be created by a single Man or by several together...The greater the number of people feeding the image with their feelings, the stronger it becomes... The image created by the collective thought can create colossal destructive or creative potential. (p. 151)

Prayer, when done with pure intent, is the voice of love that brings us internal peace, understanding, and the wisdom about how to care, and collective prayer has creative potential. I hoped that prayers being said for Mom all over the world would connect her with all those who loved her, connect her to the Divine, and raise her vibration and inner knowing that she was love. In addition I knew the prayers were going out into the hologram of consciousness to be received by others as well. The responses to my prayer requests for Mom were wonderful and I am very grateful for all the prayers. When I told a dear family friend about the gift of Mom reciting the Hail Mary that Tuesday morning, he said he would put the words to the song "Hail Mary, Gentle Woman" in the mail so I could read them to Mom.

My own prayer Wednesday morning and every morning after was to let go, surrender, and trust that Divine Mother-Father God would lead me through this last part of the journey with Mom. I said an invocation to open my heart to God's will, to listen with my heart, speak and act from my heart, trusting in divine order as I set the intention to be conscious, present, and aware for Mom. My experience with the breathwork during the training had been so powerful that on Wednesday morning I started 30 days of consecutive breathwork. I felt it important to give myself 45-60 minutes every day to be in touch with my feelings and do any clearing of negative emotions that I might have, so that when I was with Mom I would be bringing only the positive energies of compassion, harmony, peace, and love into her space. The breathwork would also help me maintain my own high vibration, something that I had promised I would do for myself.

The energy or vibration that people bring into the room of the dying person plays a role in the dying process. For example, both the Bardo and the Vedas teach that those people who are physically in the room with the person making their transition should not cry and grieve because it confuses the soul and may pull the soul back into the body rather than let it be released into the higher astral planes. My goal was to create a sacred space around Mom that was holy and safe so she and everyone in the room would feel protected on the journey. I wanted the space to be filled with happiness, love, joy, and peace, so I wanted to be sure my emotions of grief and loss were kept out of her room. How many times had I heard that "to achieve peace, you have to be peace?" If I wanted to create a peaceful environment for Mom, then I needed to be peace. Doing the breathwork during all of Mom's last thirteen days and beyond turned out to be a gift I gave to myself (and Mom). Not only were these sessions an important part of my own self-care, they also helped me gain many more insights into the journey my mother and I were taking together.

My intention for the breath session that first Wednesday was to give myself permission to relax and feel the sadness about Mom. I cried and released tremendous grief. I felt a stabbing pain in my heart from front to back, and I realized how much betrayal I felt from the nursing home staff with whom I'd advocated so hard for keeping Mom safe. I felt angry that Mom's fall was the result of being left alone in her wheel chair.

As I felt my anger with the nursing staff I experienced pain on the left side of my head around my temple, eye socket, and throat, and I interpreted it as a message for me to see the whole picture with Mom clearly and communicate my feelings in a healthy way. The affirmations that came from the session were: I assist Mom in transitioning joyfully with ease and grace. I express my anger in a healthy way. I ask for what I need.

This resulted in me sending an email to the social worker on the 4th floor of the nursing home stating that I would appreciate it if someone from the nursing home were to come by during the next couple of days and not only apologize to Mom, but ask for her forgiveness for not keeping her safe and for all the stress and ramifications her physical, emotional, psychological, and spiritual bodies had been through as a result of the neglect and subsequent fall. The email allowed me to release my anger in a healthy way. I knew that the nursing home wasn't staffed to be able to watch Mom 24/7. But I've also been trained that forgiveness during the dying process is an important part of the soul's preparation for moving into the Light—asking for forgiveness for one's transgressions, forgiving others for their transgressions against you, and forgiving the self. On a spiritual level, I also knew that everything happens as part of a Divine plan and that the fall and fractured hip were part of the Divine plan for Mom.

When I arrived in Mom's room about 11:00 am Wednesday, she was showing some signs of agitation. Her brow was furrowed and she was picking at the sheets, so I asked her nurse to come in to evaluate her for pain and anxiety. I gave Mom a kiss, told her I loved her and let her know that she was safe, but she didn't respond to my touch or words. I noted that the priest from hospice had left his card on the bed stand, and I was grateful to know that he had been there to anoint Mom again.

Mom's room still felt cold and chaotic, and my intuition told me there was negative energy in the room that needed to be cleared. My experience of working and being in hospitals and nursing homes is that they turn the rooms around fairly quickly. A new patient might be in a room less than an hour after the prior patient leaves. The only cleaning that is done is physical cleaning by housekeeping—washing down the bed, putting on clean sheets, washing the floor, the bathroom, etc. No one thinks about the energy that has been left by the people who were just in the room. Given the feel of the room I had to wonder if previous patients in the room had been afraid of dying or if they had experienced a lot of physical, emotional, psychological or spiritual suffering. Had any of the patients or their visitors been frustrated, angry or depressed? Had their loved ones been overwhelmed with fear or grief? Chances were good that a lot of negative emotions were affecting the energy in the room as the vibration in the area did *not* feel warm, peaceful, or loving. I didn't want lower vibrational energies to be attracted to the room so I wanted to clear out whatever lower vibrational energies were already there. I didn't sense any entities in the room, but sometimes when the soul leaves the body, it gets lost and doesn't go directly into the Light or a higher astral plane. In such a situation a soul may continue to hang around after it leaves the body. Vedic (Hindu) teachings say that the soul hovers around familiar places for three days. That is why in the Hindu religion, one is not cremated until three days after death.

I explained to Mom that I wanted to bring in loving peaceful energy into her room and I set to work. It's said that hearing is the last sense to leave and that it's very important to show respect in what and how you say anything when around the semi-conscious or comatose person, so as I went about working on the room's energy I talked out loud to Mom explaining to her what I was doing. Before setting out to create sacred space in the room, I took time to create sacred space in my own heart. I asked the Holy Spirit, Mary, the Magdalene, and Kwan Yin to fill and surround me with light and love and I asked for spiritual guidance for creating the sacred space for Mom to transition. Then I began using the metaphysical tools I had learned.

One clearing technique I used involved Reiki energy. The attunements I received to be a First Degree Reiki Master allowed me to clear away negative energies as well as channel healing energies into spaces. I used Reiki to do this in Mom's room, especially in the four corners. In subtle energy courses I had learned that where corners of the wall and ceiling come together at right angles, there are portals to other dimensions, and people who have pre-death experiences report that the angels and departed loved ones often appear in the upper corners of their rooms. So I wanted to be sure the corners were clean and had positive energy in them in case spiritual beings or departed loved ones came to visit Mom.

In studying other cultures, I knew that Native Americans often smudge (burn sacred plants or wood) with sage or sweet grass and that the indigenous people in South America often smudge with Palo Santo also known as Holy or Sacred Wood for cleansing heavy energy. In the Catholic and Hindu religions incense is often burned for cleansing. However, since smudging is not allowed in most nursing homes, hospitals, or hospice units I spritzed with the White Angelica™. Sage and Palo Santo are available in essential oils and can also be spritzed to clear energy and create sacred space.

I spritzed a mixture of White Angelica™ essential oil mixed with distilled water in the four corners of the room and invoked any lost souls to go into the Light, to learn about love and being loved. White Angelica™ is a blend of oils created and sold by Young Living.[6] Young Living's literature states, "White Angelica™ is a calming and soothing blend that encourages feelings of protection and security. It combines oils used during ancient times to enhance the body's aura, which brings about a sense of strength and endurance. Many people use it as protection against negative energy." The oil is a combination of geranium, spruce, myrrh, ylang ylang, hyssop, bergamot, melissa, sandalwood, rose, and rosewood oils in an almond oil base. In addition to spritzing the room I would spritz Mom with the White Angelica™ every day.

After spritzing I set an energy vortex in the room with its tail leading out the window. Vortex is defined as a place where energy goes in and/or out of a system be it the Earth (vortexes such as found in Sedona, AZ), our body (the chakras and acupuncture points) or the Universe (galaxies, black holes and white holes). According to science whenever energy moves it will move in a spiraling way, hence the name vortex that comes from the Latin word for spiraling, vertere. In creating the vortex I drew imaginary lines into the center of the room from the four corners of the ceiling and the four corners of the floor. Where the eight lines met is where I intentionally created the spiraling energy of the vortex by imagining a whirling or spiraling column of energy spinning counter clock-clockwise that was moving negative energy out the window. I invoked (called to God asking) that any intentional or unintentional non-virtuous energy that anyone brought into the room be it by thought, word, behavior, using cell phones, etc. would immediately go out the vortex and be transmuted by the Violet Flame to healing, transforming, virtuous energy to be used by Mother Earth. I further invoked that only healing, transforming virtuous energy surround and flow through Mom at all times.

---
[6] www.youngliving.com

Essential oils are also useful in raising the vibrational energy in and around patients. I set up an ultrasonic diffuser that diffused frankincense oil mixed with distilled water for 15 seconds every 50 seconds. At home I had intuitively selected frankincense from all my essential oils to bring for Mom. "Frankincense has a sweet, warm, balsamic aroma that is stimulating and elevating to the mind. Useful for visualizing, improving one's spiritual connection, and centering, it has comforting properties that help focus the mind and overcome stress and despair. Frankincense is considered the holy anointing oil in the Middle East, where it has been used in religious ceremonies for thousands of years." [7] Worwood's book states that frankincense "aligns with the spiritual; a 'calling' perfume. To call upon the divine orders, and to send love and prayers. Also for protective elements. To assist in keeping the heart pure and full of understanding." Frankincense was well known during the time of Christ for its anointing and healing powers.

I also put an orange light bulb in a lamp that I left on day and night because I had learned in studying the Bardo and the Reiki Phowa that the orange color provides a deep sense of serene detachment and energetic release from emotional objects. In his book <u>The Complete Ascension Manual: How to Achieve Ascension in this Lifetime</u>, Joshua Stone wrote, "The orange light stimulates the brain centers which causes the kundalini to flow upward." This encourages the soul and kundalini, or spiritual energy, to exit from the crown chakra, or at minimum, the third eye at the time of death.

As I continued to clear the room I noticed that someone had left several issues of People Magazine laying on the table. In my study of subtle energy, I learned that print material not only contains the energy/vibration of what is printed, but the

---

[7] www.youngliving.com

energy of the writers, publishers, etc., so I took the magazine to the family room down the hall and cleared the vibration of the magazines from the room. I made a conscious decision that the only material I would bring to read in Mom's room would be spiritual material.

Music also has vibration. There is no faster way to create or change moods than to alter the music in a room. If you doubt this think about how you feel emotionally and physically when you hear rock or rap music versus classical or soft New Age music. Science and medicine are both proving that rock and rap have much lower vibrations than classical music. We know that music using certain types of rhythm and tones can bring about a state of relaxation and physical calm. Psychology and brain researchers have found that certain music can bring about the alpha wave patterns that are associated with relaxation and mindfulness, a sense of wellbeing and joy. There is also music now that elicits the theta wave patterns that allow the listener to have subconscious insights and connect more with their spiritual selves. With this in mind I brought my CD player and played several CDs with music of higher vibration such as an instrumental of Franz Shubert's Ave Maria, a CD with chantrums that called in all the arch angels, and a couple of other CDs created to induce relaxation and a sense of peace. I had the different CDs playing almost all of the time that I was with Mom. When I'd leave at night, I put on the Ave Maria CD that would play for a little over an hour. Then there would be stillness in the room until I returned the next morning.

My intention was to create a sacred space not only for Mom to do what she had to do on all levels of her being (physical, emotional, mental, and spiritual) in order to transition from her physical body into the Light, but also so the staff and those who came to visit Mom would feel and honor the sacredness of the space, feel the tranquility, and that their vibrations would also be raised. A couple of staff members came into the room to tend to Mom shortly after I finished clearing out the lower vibrational energies and had filled it with healing Reiki energy and the higher vibrational energy of the Frankincense oil. The Ave Maria was playing softly and they commented about how peaceful the room was. I was then, and am still, very grateful to the staff for allowing me to create a sacred space for Mom, and then for honoring that space. Later in the week one of the staff said, "I wish all families would do this for their loved ones."

From this point on, the staff respected my request to keep the door to Mom's room closed. It helped to protect Mom from the disruptive energies outside her room such as fear, guilt, grief, and anger from other patients who were calling out or from patients' family members having angry outbursts at the staff. Every day as I opened the door and crossed the threshold to Mom's room, it felt like I was entering a different dimension of time and space. Some other people reported feeling the same way.

During the time I was energetically clearing the room, the Eucharistic minister came in and I received the Eucharist or Communion for Mom and me. This became part of our morning routine. To me receiving the sacrament of the Eucharist is not receiving the body of Christ as I was taught growing up in the Catholic schools. Instead, it is a reminder that we all have the Christ energy of unconditional love, compassion, and forgiveness within us. Receiving Communion helps me connect with the Christ Consciousness within myself. For me that is the energy of Light and Love and the truth of the oneness of all. Every day when I received Communion, I set the intention that it was for both Mom and me and that it would help us open our hearts to receive and be unconditional love.

Most of my days were spent sitting next to the bed holding

Mom's hand, touching her shoulder, stroking her hair, putting moisturizer on her lips, kissing her, telling her how much I loved her, and giving her permission to transition. I also would quiet my mind and consciously hold the vibration of love, compassion, appreciation, forgiveness and gratitude in my heart with the intention of sending those energies to Mom for her heart to entrain to those higher vibrations. Mainly, it was a lot of quiet time except for the music and the occasional staff member coming in.

My sister came to visit in the evening and shared an incredible experience she'd had with Mom two days earlier at the hospital. Mary Anne got off the elevator on Mom's floor and heard alarms going off. When she entered Mom's room, which was only two rooms down from the elevator, she found the alarms were going off and there was no staff present. Mom, in an apparently delirious state had pulled all the leads (cords to the heart monitor) off her chest, had them wrapped around her neck, and her face was swollen and red. I was in tears when I heard the story. In a state of delirium, had Mom wanted out of her physical suffering so much that she could have killed herself? Had she been aware on an unconscious level of what she was doing? I knew it was Divine intervention that Mary Anne arrived exactly when she did. The story was also an affirmation that I had made the right decision not to put Mom through the surgery and to transfer her from that hospital to the IPU.

The story of Mary Anne finding Mom with the cords wrapped around her neck reminded me of a dream I'd had late June, just two months previous to Mom's fall. It didn't feel like a dream as it happened in a matter of seconds. In the dream I walked up to a small group of people who stood facing me. There was a man on my left who looked familiar, but I didn't recognize him. On my right was Mom and slightly behind her was a teacher of mine, YC. I went to hug Mom, then YC. Before

I hugged YC she stepped back and there was Dad. I gave him a hug. He was all boney. He didn't hug me back. YC said Dad tried to commit suicide. I was shocked. Dad said he'd be back in a month or so as he had to go with the man. Both Mom and Dad looked like they were in their early 80s. I remember waking up puzzled. I had only had a couple of dreams about Dad since he died in 2002. Why was I dreaming about him now? My brother always said that Dad told him he had never thought about suicide, not even during the dark nights of his soul when he was in his deepest depression. Since linear time does not exist anymore for Dad, was he already aware of Mom's frail physical condition and wrapping the leads/cords around her neck? Was Dad communicating to me through my dream and giving me a warning?

CHAPTER 7

Giving and Receiving Love, Peace, Joy, and Harmony

When I arrived Thursday morning the ecumenical minister had already been there and left a white plastic rosary lying on top of Mom's hands. It pleased me to see it there as saying the Rosary always meant so much to her up until the last six months when she could no longer remember the prayers. The Rosary had always been important in our family. We often said the Rosary as a family during Lent or Advent, and I even remember the family saying the Rosary over Mom's abdomen when she was pregnant with my brother. With those memories playing through my mind I decided I'd say the Rosary out loud to Mom every morning. After that it became part of our daily morning spiritual ritual together, and on some level I knew she was hearing and receiving the vibration of the prayers.

That morning before I left home, I'd also felt drawn to bring a bottle of Light Being Master Essence Oil from Germany. The oil I brought was labeled #5 and was calibrated to the energetic vibrational pattern of the Christ Consciousness energy that is pure, unconditional love. The oil is supposed to heal on a soul level and work directly to release blockages on the energetic systems of the body, to bring a feeling of comfort and all encompassing love. I was guided to anoint Mom's heart, third eye, and crown chakras with it every morning. I also did the same for myself. Following the anointing, I would check Mom's chakras to be sure they were all open and clear, and illuminate them by bringing healing light into her chakras so that divine energy was flowing through her.

I did this as Eastern, Egyptian and shamanic traditions teach that each chakra is a door through which the soul can depart. For all traditions the goal is for healing to be completed in all chakras so they are clear and the soul exists through the crown chakra. According to Inca shamanic legend, when all the chakras are clear, one acquires a "rainbow body" and is ready to die consciously and make the journey beyond death to the Spirit world.

One of my soul sisters, Lucy, who is an ordained metaphysician, came by in the late morning. She said that during her meditation that morning she was guided to come do a special healing on Mom. She also checked Mom's chakras and found them to be open and illuminated. After Lucy completed her healing and anointing, we worked together to put a protective shield around Mom's aura to allow her to do her inner work in peace with grace and ease. As we were finishing up a nurse came in to give Mom her Dilaudid so she would be comfortable for her next repositioning. The nurse commented about how peaceful the room felt and how peaceful Mom seemed to be. On her way out she said, "I'll let the two of you get back to your voodoo. Whatever you're doing, it works." Lucy and I just smiled at each other. Even though the nurse didn't know how to express it she could feel the energetic difference in the room. Lucy came a couple more times during Mom's stay on IPU to visit and give her metaphysical healings for her soul's journey.

In the afternoon while Mom was resting peacefully, I did my breathwork. My intention was to rest and allow whatever needed to come up to do so. I felt alive, my heart beating regular and strong. I allowed myself to simply be in the present moment and appreciate the gift of this journey with Mom. At one point I realized I had synchronized my breathing to hers and felt myself breathing in courage and strength for her to make her transition fearlessly and peacefully. I became aware that I wanted to be out of my body traveling on the astral with her, and I had to keep grounding myself. What came to me was the understanding that Mom carried me (birthed me) into this physical world and I was carrying her to the gates of heaven and out of this physical world—birthing her back into the Light in a way similar to the image from my first mandala. My affirmation for the session was, "I carry Mom to the gates of heaven where she is birthed into the Light."

The next day began with our wonderful morning ritual. I said the Rosary out loud to Mom, anointed her with the Christ oil, received Communion for both of us, and said prayers with the Eucharistic minister. When I started the second decade of the Rosary, saying, "Hail Mary, full of grace," I was suddenly overcome with emotion and tears of love for Mom. I was aware that Mom was filling up with grace, the gift of love and spiritual healing from Divine Mother-Father God. I had a sense of all the prayers sent to her twinkling on the Divine Matrix and I could also sense them going into her crown chakra, filling her entire being with grace and love. I could see Mom as a perfect being, full of grace and aligned with Divine Mother-Father God, and I had to stop and tell her how beautiful she was and how she was filled with grace just like the Virgin Mary. I held that vision of Mom every day, and each day I told her how beautiful she was, perfect in the eyes of God and filled with grace.

I was also aware that the sacred space was multidimensional. It felt to me like there was an inner and outer energy system. The outer energy was generated by the higher vibrations of the oils, the music, the vortex, and the orange light that all worked together to raise the energy levels in Mom's physical body so she would be more comfortable as her body was dying. The inner spiritual energy system was made up of the prayers, meditations, and invocations that were being sent to her from all over the world, helping her subconsciously to release old, unhealthy beliefs about death and dying and helping her soul prepare to go into the Light. Together the outer and inner energy systems were providing complete sustenance to her physical, emotional, psychological, and spiritual bodies.

The other awareness was that the sacred space was not just the room. A sacred space had also been created in both of our hearts. I felt an amazing connection between our two hearts and I could visualize our hearts as two perfect glistening white lotus blossoms with sunlight shining down on each of them. The image reminded me of purity and love, and being touched by the golden rays of God's love.

Late in the afternoon, several people from the nursing home came to visit Mom and to tell her and me they were sorry about her fall. What a lesson on visiting the dying they gave me. Unconsciously for them, but obvious to me, was the fact that they were there for their own needs, not for Mom. They spoke in loud voices, calling her name and asking if she remembered when they had done certain activities. The loudness and shift in energy aroused Mom from her peaceful, quiet, pain-free state to slight consciousness. And somewhere in her state of politeness and graciousness she managed to acknowledge their presence through a quiet noise, a change in facial expression, or a response when they touched her. Of course, they were thrilled. Excitedly they said, "She knows I'm here." However, what they weren't noticing was her furrowed brow and the signs of pain and agitation that followed, so much so that when they left I had to ask Mom's nurse to give her medication early in order to relieve her discomfort.

My guess is that most people, medically trained or not, aren't aware of the energy that it takes for the terminally ill person to die. When the organs are shutting down, there may be toxins produced that cause physical discomfort. It also takes a lot of spiritual energy to go within and make peace with oneself, with others and with God, and prepare to leave loved ones. I remember being with Mom at the nursing home when the staff wheeled in one of the residents to have lunch. I looked in his eyes and saw so much despair, anger and grief, and I sensed that this resident wanted to be left alone to die. It was obvious he didn't want to eat, as he'd purse his lips shut and turn his head. Yet the staff insisted on joking with him trying to get him to eat or drink something. No one was tuned in to his energy nor were they respecting his wishes. I thought, please leave the dear man alone and let him go back to his room and be in peace. He passed away two days later.

My observation from being around the elderly in nursing homes and hospitals is that families and staff need to be trained to listen, honor and respect what the patients are saying by word, body language, and how they are behaving. They need to be trained not to fear death, but to see it as a joyful rebirth and do everything possible to surround the patient in the higher vibrations of love, peace, harmony, and joy to better facilitate their transition into the Light.

Early that evening, after the visitors departed, my brother Patrick arrived from California. My sister came over so all three of us were with Mom. Patrick's wife would arrive the next day and I wondered if Mom would choose to make her transition when all three of her children were with her.

When I got home that evening I made a sign to post on Mom's door that stated, "Please honor the sacred space that Mary is in to make her transition. Please have conversations outside the room. Thank you, Mary's Family". I taped the sign to Mom's door the next day. I hoped it would alert visitors before they came in the room to be quiet and respectful of the sacred process that Mom was in. That evening I also had a beautiful breathwork session. My intention was to use the breath to keep myself grounded so I could be present and loving for Mom and feel the joy of our journey together. I received a beautiful movie-like vision. I was a maple tree in a grove of trees, and I was watching them grow thicker and taller during each of the four seasons and over the years. Behind me there was a dead tree that had fallen upon which lichen and moss were growing. This represented my father whose knowledge and love of botany still lives on in me. Next to me was a dying maple tree that had only one leaf left on it (my mom). It was the fall of the year and my leaves were just beginning to turn yellow, orange and red. I realized because the tree next to me was dying, more sunlight was reaching me giving my branches the nourishment needed to reach further up to the sky than the dying tree had ever grown, and it allowed me to develop more beautiful foliage. My branches were filled with singing birds and squirrels' nests. Chipmunks had burrowed in around my roots that spread underground through the entire orchard. There was incredible worm and insect activity going on in the soil around my root system. I was giving and receiving life from the animal and plant kingdoms, from Mother Earth. The visualization was a metaphor for how much the journey Mom and I have been taking together, especially the past six months, had allowed me to grow into my own spiritual and healing power. It was also a metaphor for the fact that we are part of nature and follow the same life-death cycle like all living things in nature. I felt so much love and gratitude for Mom. My affirmation was, I stand in my power, flowing, strong, growing, giving, and receiving.

Saturday marked one week since Mom had fallen and broken her hip. The envelope from our friend in California with the words to "Hail Mary, Gentle Woman" was in the mail when I arrived home Friday night. I read them to Mom Saturday morning after I said the Rosary and this also became part of our morning spiritual ritual. I would read them to her a couple more times during the day because the words were so beautiful and the refrain was a perfect reflection of how I was feeling about her:

"Hail Mary, Gentle Woman"
Intro: Cantor
Hail Mary, full of grace, the Lord is with you.
Blessed are you among women, and
Blessed is the fruit of your womb, Jesus.
Holy Mary, Mother of God,
Pray for us sinners now,
and at the hour of death. Amen.
Refrain: All
Gentle woman, quiet light, morning star
so strong and bright,
gentle mother peaceful dove
teach us wisdom; teach us love.
Verse: All
You were chosen by the Father:
You were chosen for the Son,
You were chosen from all women
and for woman shining one.
Refrain: All
Gentle woman, quiet light, morning star
so strong and bright
gentle mother peaceful dove
teach us wisdom; teach us love.

Verse: All
Blessed are you among women
Blessed in turn all women too
Blessed they with peaceful spirits
Blessed they with gentle hearts.
Refrain: All
Gentle woman, quiet light, morning star
so strong and bright
gentle mother peaceful dove
teach us wisdom; teach us love.
(Carey Landry)

Before I left home Saturday morning, I was drawn to smell Young Living's Peace & Calming® essential oil. After smelling it I decided to alternate the Peace & Calming® with the frankincense in the diffuser every other day. The fragrant ingredients of tangerine, orange, ylang ylang, patchouli and blue tansy, are relaxing, uplifting and encourage a peaceful state, and the nurses always loved coming into Mom's room. Once when I was sitting next to Mom I heard the door open and turned to find a nurse standing there taking in a deep breath her arms slowly and gently rising and lowering with each inhale and exhale. She looked at me and said, "I feel totally relaxed and peaceful when I come in this room." She then turned around and walked out. It wasn't just the essence of the essential oils that the nurse was feeling. It was also the energy vibration of the sacred space.

Patrick came by that morning and later went to the airport to pick up his wife, Madeline. My sister came over later in the afternoon and my husband came over right before dinner. We all took turns sitting by Mom and holding her hand, stroking her hair, and talking gently to her. I found it a little harder to stay fully present in the moment with Mom when there were several people in the room. When quiet conversations started about memories, I was able to consciously visualize any hints of negative energy being drawn through the vortex I had created and out through the window. I realized how wonderful having the vortex was as it eliminated the necessity of me having to police every conversation, cell phone call, text message that brought discordant energy into the room.

I could feel that the vortex was not only pulling out negative thoughts, emotions, and words that were being said at any given moment, but that, at least for me, it was drawing away past hurts and grievances. I found it so much easier to forgive Mom and myself for our past transgressions against each other and this allowed me to focus on the moment and to be present to the divine energies and the divine process of Mom's transition.

The next day I reflected on the fact that during the week several of the nurses told me that when patients are as peaceful as Mom, they often "slip out" without giving any warning signs to the staff or family. I think the nurses were trying to prepare me with the knowledge that death doesn't always happen the way we would like it to. As much as I hoped to be with Mom when she transitioned, I knew it was her soul's choice. Since I didn't know when she might transition and who else might be there, I decided I would start reading aloud privately to Mom a version of one of the passages that I learned from "The Great Liberation Through Hearing" in the Bardo, or Tibetan Book of the Dead. I felt that this was the best way to honor my siblings' wishes at the time of our Mom's death, as I knew they might not be comfortable with me saying the Bardo right after Mom died if we were all there together. The purpose of reading "The Great Liberation Through Hearing" to Mom was to place her in the right state of mind as she approached death and to help her practice leaving her physical body and have her soul make its journey into the Light.

For me this prayer, like saying the Rosary and having people pray for her, was uniting Mom with many beautiful souls across cultures and time, and it provided yet another avenue for raising Mom's vibratory rate. While this prayer is from the Bardo, my belief is that God is Light (1 John 4:8) and God is Love (1 John 1:5) and that by calling upon God as Light and Love those aspects of God would be compelled to move towards Mom and carry her into the Divine Mother/Father God's spiritual realm. Thus, I also hoped it would open her consciousness to the fact that she could and should merge with Light and Love. So, from that Sunday through the day Mom transitioned, I read the following prayer from the Bardo to her two or three times a day, repeating it several times at each reading:

> Mom, go forth into the Light. Hold fast to it. Feel yourself engulfed in the blaze of the White Light. Let go. Rise up from your body. Leave it lying deserted like a worn out garment. Allow yourself to float up into the down-reaching Light.
>
> Melt into the glow of Love. Peace! Peace! Peace! Think not of the past. Banish all regrets. Leave all old memories behind. Discard all apprehensions. Remember the Light!
>
> Do not be distracted, Mom. Turn your full concentration upward toward the White Light.
>
> Feel it immerse your entire being. Absorb it. You are floating free and light. You are moving upward into Love."[8]

Mom and I had our morning spiritual ritual alone together before other family members arrived. I didn't know if it was

---

[8] Christman, p. 102

from reading the Bardo prayer to Mom or not, but my limbs were tingly, my heart felt too light, my breathing was a little stressed—almost as if it I was the one going through the death process. I had to work to keep myself grounded. I was also sensing that the room was a multi-dimensional, timeless space. I frequently experienced a feeling of oneness, of being carried or held and wrapped in loving energy. The experiences made me wonder if I was sensing the presence of angelic and/or spiritual beings in the room. Every day I had asked my brother Kevin and my mother's mother, Sarah to be with us, and particularly with Mom during her journey Home. I was certainly feeling someone's loving presence and support.

Patrick left early Sunday afternoon to go back to California and a very busy work schedule. Before he departed, he took some time alone with Mom to create whatever closure they needed with each other. Patrick said that he felt complete with Mom and would come back after Mom made her transition.

Sunday evening I intuitively heard that I should start putting rose petals on Mom's bed. There was one red rose remaining in a small floral arrangement in the room, so I gently scattered its petals on her bed.

On Monday when I went to purchase roses and saw the variety of colors, I immediately knew they had to be pink, and I bought a dozen beautiful, pink roses so there would be enough to put rose petals on Mom's bed and pillow every day. I chose pink because even though the heart chakra is traditionally green, when I envision it I see a light pink, tinged on the outside with a pale green. Choosing the pink petals was another validation to me that Mom's and my heart chakras were open and connected with each other.

When I'd arrived home Sunday evening I was curious about why my intuition had told me to use rose petals and not petals from another flower. I Googled rose flower essence and found that rose flower essence has a healing quality, and it particularly affects one at the emotional level. It soothes and balances the nervous system and supports and protects the heart from emotional pain and trauma. The rose is supposed to have the highest vibration of all the flowers, vibrating at around 800, and also represents the divine mother. I wondered if the vibration of the rose petals would be another resource in the outer energy system to help Mom be able to leave her family in the physical plane with ease, grace, and free of trauma.

When the Eucharistic minister came that morning her voice kept cracking while she was saying the prayers because she was trying not to cry. That day was the first day with the pink rose petals on Mom's bed and pillow. Tearfully, she said, "I've never seen anything so beautiful. She is so peaceful."

Once the Bardo prayer was added to our morning spiritual ritual, the ritual remained the same and continued until Mom died. The only thing that changed was that a different Eucharistic minister came each day. Every morning I would have to stop at some point during the Rosary or the "Hail Mary, Gentle Woman" and allow the tears of gratitude to flow for the healing transforming prayers we were receiving and for feeling so supported and wrapped in love by the spiritual beings in the room. I would hold the vision that Mom was a flawless being, full of grace and aligned with the perfection seen in her by the Blessed Mother Mary and by Divine Mother-Father God. I would tell Mom how beautiful and filled with grace she was, and I always felt this was one of the highest vibrational points of our days together. It was such a blessing to start our days together wrapped in light, love, grace, and the feeling of oneness with all.

Madeline came in that day after Mom and I had our morning ritual, and I left them alone for a while. Apparently Madeline had wonderful closure with Mom, as Patrick told me later in the week that at one point Mom lifted her arm as if reaching up to Madeline. I could feel things drawing to a close as each of us found our peace with Mom.

Every day I continued painting visual landscapes of heaven in my quiet one-way conversations with Mom. On Monday while some music was playing with sounds of nature in the background I had a vision that I shared with her. I said, "Mom, I'm imagining that when you get to heaven you will find everyone, including yourself is healthy and whole. I'm envisioning you, Dad, and Kevin (my brother who died when he was 17 months old) going for a walk in the woods. Kevin is skipping ahead of you and Dad. Dad is finding morels and other wonderful edible mushrooms and Kevin is pulling up wild onions and bringing them to you so you can have wild onion and peanut butter sandwiches (one of her favorite sandwiches). It's going to be wonderful Mom." Every day I'd also tell her it was okay to go whenever she was ready; that we all wanted her to be at peace, to go Home into the Light into unconditional love, and to be with everyone who would be waiting there for her. I'd assure her that we would all be okay.

Tuesday was a more difficult day for Mom as she wasn't in that usual peaceful state she had been in for so many days. Mom had been off all fluids, including IVs for a week. Her urine output was minimal and very concentrated and she was getting smaller every day as the fluids left her body and her organs began shutting down. In spite of this her respirations and pulse were within normal limits and her lungs were clear. Unfortunately the medication didn't seem to be holding her comfortably for as long as it had and she showed signs of pain when she was even slightly repositioned in the bed. Her brow was furrowed much of the day and she was groaning. Her eyes were shifting back and forth underneath her closed eyelids and I wondered if she was having her end-of-life review, seeing her life pass before her prior to her physical death. A couple of times her eyes very slightly opened and she put her left arm out as if reaching for something or someone. Was she seeing or sensing the presence of a spiritual being or a loved one? Only she knew. Up until that day, and then afterwards, her eyes were still and there was no movement behind her eyelids.

I'd worked with the nursing staff all day to try to keep Mom comfortable. Finally I asked the hospice doctor to observe Mom being turned so she could see what I was observing as far as pain. The doctor increased the Dilaudid from .5 mg to 2 mg half an hour before Mom was turned and ordered the Intensol to be given every four hours. I was grateful that I could relax a little and not have to be as vigilant monitoring Mom's body language to know when to ask for the medication. Again, pain management is so important in helping the patient stay calm and peaceful and keeping them from going into fearful negative thinking. Plus I knew that Mom's choice her whole life was to take medication to help alleviate physical pain, so I respected that during her transition process. I also honor that some cultures and major religions of the world have teachings about redemptive suffering and that selecting pain management is the patient's choice based on personal beliefs. If possible, family members should be aware of their loved one's wishes regarding medical treatment and pain control. It is very important that the person holding the patient's Power of Attorney know their wishes, especially in cases like my mom's where she was no longer able to verbally communicate her wishes to us.

During the previous week my physical body often needed a break from sitting in unusual positions that allowed me to be hold Mom's hand or touch her to maintain some form of physical contact with her. When I'd need a break, I would go to the family room to eat whatever food I brought or I would sit back and work on the baby blanket I was knitting. I love to use knitting as a form of japa (continual repetition of a mantra either silently or out loud). As I'd knit each stitch I'd say a word in a mantra. So it took four stitches to say *Shanti, Shanti, Shanti, Om,* a mantra I recited for peace in my heart, Mom's heart, the hearts of all those in the hospice unit, and the hearts of all sentient beings in the world. The other mantra I'd recite in my head was *Lokah Samastah Sukhino Bhavantu,* a traditional Hindu prayer that translates, *May all the beings in all the worlds be peaceful and happy.* Doing japa while knitting also helped raised the vibrational energy in the room, in both of our bodies as well as in the bodies of all those who came into the room. I considered it a spiritual gift I could give to the hospice staff, to family, and those visiting Mom. It was interesting to me that I was knitting a blanket for a baby being born into this physical world while I was being present for Mom to be born into the spiritual world. I thought, the baby receiving this blanket is going to be wrapped in so much peace and love.

When I got home in the evening I had a beautiful breathwork session with the intention that I allow the breath to take me wherever I need to go. All my chakras were open and sparkling and I felt tremendous gratitude for all those who were supporting Mom and our family on this journey, and I felt so blessed by the gift that Mom was in my life and the sense of completion I felt with her. I was also so very aware of how everything I had learned the past six years had led to my creating and holding this sacred space for our time together. My affirmation was, I am filled with gratitude for Mom and this journey together.

The next day was Wednesday and I was finding it difficult to watch Mom's body get smaller and frailer every day. I had more respect and honor for the process of letting go of one's physical body and I loved her more and more. From this day on, Mom's body became totally flaccid as if she was in a coma and her urine output ceased during the night shift.

Some time during Wednesday I had what I call a down pouring of wisdom from one of my spiritual guides. I was to breathe in the Holy Spirit through my crown chakra and on the exhale blow from Mom's feet up through all of her chakras while I held the intention that I was breathing the Holy Spirit through her body to unite the vibrations of her grace and love with that of Divine Light and love so that her soul could leave and become one with God. I never question these messages or insights that I receive, so I did this several times a day until Mom transitioned. My heart chakra felt open and I felt attuned to higher angelic spiritual beings even though I wasn't outwardly seeing or hearing anyone.

When I was saying the Rosary the next morning, I received the spiritual message that this journey with Mom was an initiation for me. At first I had no idea what the initiation was for, and then it came to me. Mom and I were completing our karma or all our life's contracts with each other. I was teaching her about love, loving and being loved unconditionally. I was showing her the path Home. Her fall and breaking her hip was her gift to me as it allowed me to open my heart completely, to release and surrender to God's guidance on this journey with Mom, to trust my intuition and to see that this work might be my next career path. What greater love could there be than for a mother to give her life for her child? She was one of my greatest teachers. Tears of gratitude flowed down my cheeks.

Mom had no urine output at all on Thursday so her kidneys had definitely shut down. I asked a nurse how long someone could survive after the kidneys shut down. She replied, "It varies from patient to patient. It may be days. Why would your mom want to leave this space you created where there is so much peace and love?" I hoped the space wasn't so comfortable that Mom's soul didn't feel able to leave her physical body. But from her first day in the hospice unit I had assured her that it was okay to go, and I had told her all of us, my siblings, our children and her great granddaughter, wanted and were praying for her to be in peace and to go to the Light.

When I got home that night I had an amazing breathwork session. My intention was to allow the breath to take me where I needed to heal. I started wondering why it was taking Mom's soul so long to go home. I was sure Mom really loved all the nurturing she was getting, but I also knew the soul chooses how and when it leaves the physical body. My chest became heavy and I was overwhelmed with sadness and tears as I had a vision of Kevin dying.

When my brother Kevin died at 17 months old, my father was working in a different state and my mom was alone with my sister and Kevin. My mom sat in the rocking chair and watched him die in his crib. She was either afraid to hold him while he died or didn't know that she could. I had been focused on wanting to be with her when she transitioned and on showing her in this lifetime that dying is something beautiful. One doesn't have to be afraid of touching and holding a dying person. All of the sudden I realized that Kevin's soul also chose how it was going to depart. It was an "ah hah" moment for me. I had felt anger with Mom for so many years that she hadn't held Kevin while he was dying. I had felt his loneliness. But, in that "ah hah" moment, I completely forgave Mom and felt so much compassion for both her and Kevin. I released my anger with Mom and forgave myself for being angry with her for so many years. She truly hadn't known what to do. My heart felt fuller and lighter and I was so grateful that I was doing breathwork during this journey with Mom. My affirmation was, I am at peace with however Mom's soul transitions into Light and Love. I also thanked Kevin for bringing this awareness to me.

He was there with me helping Mom transition.

We had arranged for the hospice music-thanatologist to come on Friday at about 9:30 am to play the harp and (vocally) tone for Mom. In simplest terms, a music-thanatologist is a highly skilled musician-clinician with specialized education and/or certification in working with the dying and bereaved. The primary goal of music-thanatology is "to lovingly serve the physical and spiritual needs of the dying through the delivery of *prescriptive music* . . .. With voice and harp, often but not always in teams of two, the music is delivered live at the bedside of each dying person, it is individualize, customized, and these medical deliveries of sonic medicine are termed: *vigils* (from the Latin: alert)."[9] The music-thanatologist came in and sat quietly with Mom. My sense was that he was connecting with Mom and assessing what her physical, emotional, and spiritual needs were so that the music he created and delivered met her individual needs at that moment and would provide her comfort on the different levels of her being. I felt he was musically ministering to Mom.

My sister and I were honored to both be sitting on either side of Mom and holding her hands during the session. The music-thanatologist would play the harp, then tone vocally. There would be silence for a moment and then he would play and tone again. I could see that he was attuned to Mom's energy. I felt connected to Mom's heart and soul. The music was also touching and healing my heart and soul and the tears ran down my cheeks. The hour went by quickly and though Mom showed no visible response during the session I knew it was a beautiful gift. I could only imagine that her soul's vibrational level was getting higher and higher. In my imagination the angelic beings in the room were toning and playing their own

---

[9] Schroeder-Sheker, p. 15

harps in concert with the harp of the music-thanatologist.

My breathwork that night brought another gift from the day. My intention was to explore the pain I was experiencing on the left side in my lower abdomen. What came to me was that it felt like ovarian pain even though I no longer have my ovaries. That vision took me to one of being an egg developing inside my mother when she was a fetus inside her mother, and I could see the energetic connection across three generations. I appreciated how the mother-child bond and symbiotic connection in the womb is the closest two people can ever get. I also appreciated how hard it must have been for my mother to look different from the other children at school because of her birthmark and to lose her mother when she was only 13. I had images of Mom as a healthy 4-5 year old running outside and playing with her parents on the lawn on the farm, and then I had an image of her sitting on her father's lap eating dinner, and being teased but loved by her five older brothers. I also came to the realization that once Mom transitioned I would be no one's child, not a child, a grandchild, or a godchild. I felt very sad as the reality sunk in that I would soon be the oldest generation. But with that realization also came the knowing that the healing work Mom and I were doing in our hearts, the resolution of our karmas and contracts, and the insights I was having about the dying process, were healing generations backwards and forwards, not just Mom and me. I had two affirmations: "Mom and I are both healers," and "I am healthy, whole, young and vibrant."

On Saturday I did my breathwork in the morning before visiting Mom. My intention was to use the breath to check my chakras for any possible blockages regarding my relationship with her. Were there any unresolved issues between us that might be preventing her from transitioning?

In my first chakra I found some roots starting to shrivel. I felt very sad seeing my Mom as the last of her family's generation pass on and felt sad that there are so few descendants in Chloe's (Mom's only great grandchild's) generation. My childhood holiday world revolved around Mom's family and I felt tremendous gratitude for my aunts and uncles. All my other chakras were clear except there was heaviness in my heart. The heaviness was about a family cut-off. When I was 14 I was molested on Easter Sunday by the husband of one of my cousins in my mother's family. My cousin and I had been estranged ever since, a period of 46 years. I received the clear message that I was to call her when Mom passed and invite her to Mom's funeral. My affirmations were, I am grateful for all the wonderful gifts I received from Mom's family and I accept with an open, loving heart all who come to honor Mom's life. I wondered if this had come to me in breathwork because my heart had been so open and filled with love, compassion and forgiveness with this journey. I did call and leave my cousin a voice message.

Patrick blessed the ending of what I knew would be Mom's final week by surprising us and flying in on Saturday to continue his support of Mom's journey. Mom was being blessed again with her three children surrounding her and loving her.

CHAPTER 8
Into the Light

Sunday morning when I opened the door to Mom's room I immediately felt chilled. The room felt much colder than ever before and I noticed that the remaining pink roses had drooped their heads. There was a definite shift of energy in the room. This was day thirteen that Mom had gone without food or water. Interestingly, to indigenous cultures the number 13 has spiritual significance and is considered to have auspicious meaning and to bring blessings and happiness. The number 13 holds prominence in indigenous ritual art, ceremonial songs, time and placement. It also becomes 4 (1+3=4) in numerology. And four represents the order of the universe and stability, like a square. I wondered if this 13th day without food or water might be an auspicious day for Mom.

I put down my purse and bag, went over to kiss Mom and let her know I was there. As I felt her hands I could feel that they were much colder than the day before. I touched her feet and they were also ice cold, but her calves were warm. There was no discoloration in her feet or hands. Her breathing and pulse were still normal and I couldn't hear any signs of fluid in her lungs. She looked very peaceful.

I started my morning ritual with her by putting on the Ave Maria CD. I took the wilted pink rose petals off her bed covers and pillow and replaced them with fresh ones. I put fresh distilled water and frankincense oil in the diffuser before I began our spiritual ritual of saying the Rosary, reading "Hail Mary, Gentle Woman," anointing Mom with the Christ oil, and reading several times the passage from the Bardo.

Patrick, Mary Anne, and Rich came at different times during the day, and each of us took turns sitting with Mom, holding her hand, stroking her hair, talking gently to her and having quiet time with her. As the day progressed I sensed a greater energetic shift happening in Mom. The cold was moving up Mom's legs, but she was at peace all day. I had a sense that Mom might transition during the night and told Rich I was going to spend the night in Mom's room.

In the evening Mary Anne and Rich left and Patrick and I were alone with Mom. We both noticed that Mom had opened her eyes just enough that they were little slits. Her right eye would blink normally. Patrick got down so he was in her line of vision, but there was no response. But her eyes stayed open just a slit and it was like she was staring at someone or something. We'll never know since she wasn't able to verbally communicate with us.

When Patrick volunteered to sit with Mom so I could rest on the couch in the room I took him up on it. Since I wasn't going home for the night and didn't know what the night might bring, I used the time to do my breath work session. My intention was to relax and restore my energy with the breathing. I started breathing and allowed my muscles to start relaxing. I envisioned Mother Mary, Mary Magdalene, and Kwan Yin ministering to me, massaging my muscles, holding me, loving me and giving me even more strength to help Mom transition, just as they had been there holding the energy for Christ when he transitioned. I wasn't able to completely tune out Mom's breathing during my session and was aware that it started becoming a little sporadic, less regular. I completed my session about 5:20 pm and Patrick and I took turns going to the family room to get a bite to eat.

In the end, the transition came quickly. A little after 9:00 pm Patrick said "What if Mom lives to be 103?" Then, my cell phone rang. It was my daughter Ashley, so I went out to the hall to give her an update on Mom.

When I came back to the room I noticed a stillness that hadn't been there before. "Patrick, listen. Mom's breath has gotten much quieter." We both watched her chest and her breath was still regular. We pulled up a second chair so we could both sit next to her. Patrick was on my right holding Mom's right hand and I was at her head looking into her face. I hand my hand over her heart chakra feeling her heart slow down, getting quieter and quieter. I told her to remember the Light, to see the White Light, to remember it was her birthright to leave her body and go Home into the down pouring Light, into the Love, into the peace, peace, perfect peace, and that she was perfect love, filled with grace. Suddenly, I could see a hint of a smile on her lips. I stroked her face and continued talking with her. She was so beautiful. Tears of joy were pouring from my eyes and it was so quiet I could hear my tears when they dropped on the bed. I prayed to keep my throat chakra open so I could keep talking and encouraging her to go Home into the Light, into the Love.

At that moment Mom's eyes opened wide and she looked directly into mine. Her eyes were so bright and there was golden white light emanating from them. Knowing the eyes are the windows to the soul, I felt that the veil between the dimensions had lifted for mom and she was glimpsing the light, love, joy and freedom of her true spiritual nature as a soul.

She was already filling with light, and I imagined she was seeing God and feeling the unconditional love. Was she conscious that she was leaving her physical body and returning to Light, returning Home to wholeness, to being her true self? After all, we aren't physical bodies with souls. We are souls who have come to earth to learn and have experiences in physical bodies. As I continued to look down at her face I saw another slight smile. Then she took a deep breath and closed her eyes. Patrick leaned over to listen to her heart, she took two more breaths and she was gone, but the slight smile remained. It was about 9:45 pm. Having Mom become aware in some way before she transitioned was an amazing gift. The miracle of this gift was that Mom had been unresponsive since September 9th and her body totally flaccid the previous five days. I believe that in the end she was conscious and aware that she was going Home, that she was going into the Light. She was grace, Light and love.

CHAPTER 9
Conscious, Deliberate Closure

Patrick and I stayed with Mom for about fifteen minutes before I went out to get a nurse to come make the pronouncement. I had immediately noticed an energetic shift in the room after Mom took her last breath. When Mom's soul left, her essence left. I wondered if her soul was carried by the angelic beings or loved ones that had been surrounding us for days. There wasn't that special spark of warmth and love in the room anymore. The room felt lonely without Mom's spirit and essence, but I couldn't have been more joyful, more at peace, or more thankful that her transition into the Light was so beautiful and peaceful.

When the nurse came in, she turned the air conditioner on full blast to keep Mom's body cold. I called Rich and he said he'd call our two children and then head down to the hospital. Patrick called Mary Anne and left to go pick her up. I stayed and sat with Mom. I asked Mom to send me a sign that she was okay. I asked for a specific sign, to see the shape of an angel in the clouds or in the negative space created by clouds.

Once we were all reassembled in Mom's room, the staff gave us all the time we needed to be with her. After we each said our good-byes, we took turns sitting with Mom while we called other family members and the funeral home. Just as Mom, Mary Anne, Patrick and Madeline had done when Dad died, we wanted to consciously be attentive to Mom's body. It had been the home for her soul for 93 years and we wanted to honor that. I asked to stay with Mom while her body was washed one last time. After they washed her, I tearfully but joyfully anointed her body one more time, gently caressing and rubbing Frankincense all over her torso, I gave her a last kiss and the aides gently dressed her in the clothes I had chosen.

Once she was dressed, we all stayed with Mom and watched while she was put into the body bag. Before we left the room, I said a prayer of gratitude for the space that held us so lovingly for thirteen days. I thanked the vortex for its healing energy. My intuition told me that I should leave the vortex in place to help all the patients and their families who would be in the room in the future. We followed the cart down to the funeral home's van and watched Mom's body being put into the van. We then followed the van to the nursing home, and once there we watched as the body was wheeled into the funeral home. At about 1:30 am on Monday morning we left the funeral home with plans to return the following morning to arrange for Mom's cremation and pick out an urn for her ashes.

At the funeral home the next morning I was pleased to see that among the selection of urns was one just like Dad's, so I picked that one for Mom. A couple of times during the day I recited the prayer from the Bardo I had said out loud to Mom so many times..

The cremation was scheduled for Tuesday morning at 8:30. I picked Mary Anne up and we arrived at the funeral home at 8:15. They immediately took us down to the crematorium and we watched as they put the cardboard box with Mom in the cremator. We went back upstairs, shared happy memories, I occasionally said the prayer from the Bardo in my head, Mary Anne read, I knitted, and a couple of times we went out and watched the heat from the cremator rise into the sky. After Dad was cremated, with permission from the rest of the family, I had taken two tablespoons of his ashes out of the urn before they were interred. Originally I thought I would scatter them on the beach in Laguna Beach, California, one of Dad's favorite places. But when I gave it more thought, I realized I should put them in a safe place and mix them with Mom's ashes when the time came, so I had I brought Dad's ashes and asked that they be mixed with Mom's. The whole cremation process took less than four hours. They brought us Mom's (and Dad's) ashes in the urn and we headed out to the car. I put the urn in the back seat and put the seat belt around it for safety, just as I had pulled a seat belt across Mom's lap over the past several years since she couldn't see to do it herself. Mary Anne and I both smiled.

The funeral Mass was at St. Giles on Saturday, September 27th, just as Mom had requested. It was a beautiful service honoring her life as a wife, mother, grandmother, friend, and needlework artist. The urn with her ashes sat in a beautiful wreath of pink rose buds and ivy. Among the songs the soloist sang was "Hail Mary, Gentle Woman". Everyone gathered afterwards for a luncheon and people got up and lovingly spoke about the impact Mom had on their lives. It was all as Mom had wished.

My brother, a cousin, and I took Mom's ashes to the cemetery on October 11th to be interred next to my father and brother. We each sprinkled the pink rose buds from the wreath around the urn before the vault holding the urn was closed. The priest offered some prayers and I read Kahlil Gibran's poem "On Death" from his 1923 book <u>The Prophet</u>:

> You would know the secret of death.
> But how shall you find it unless you seek it in the heart of life?
> The owl whose night-bound eyes are blind unto the day cannot unveil the mystery of light.
> If you would indeed behold the spirit of death, open your heart wide unto the body of life.
> For life and death are one, even as the river and the sea are one.
> In the depth of your hopes and desires lies your silent knowledge of the beyond;
> And like seeds dreaming beneath the snow your heart dreams of spring.
> Trust the dreams, for in them is hidden the gate to eternity.
> Your fear of death is but the trembling of the shepherd when he stands before the king whose hand is to be laid upon him in honour.
> Is the shepherd not joyful beneath his trembling, that he shall wear the mark of the king?
> Yet is he not more mindful of his trembling?
> For what is it to die but to stand naked in the wind and to melt into the sun?
> And what is to cease breathing, but to free the breath from its restless tides, that it may rise and expand and seek God unencumbered?
> Only when you drink from the river of silence shall you indeed sing.
> And when you have reached the mountaintop, then you shall begin to climb.
> And when the earth shall claim your limbs, then shall you truly dance.

On Sunday, October 12th, the day after interring Mom's ashes I had another mystical experience. As I was driving home from dinner with a friend, I looked up in the sky and there in the negative space created by the clouds was an angel in a flowing dress dancing on one foot, wings outstretched. I asked my friend, "What do you see?"

She said, "It's an angel."

It was the sign I'd asked Mom for. She was fine. Mom was free and dancing. We pulled off the road to watch her as she danced across the sky. It was a very special shared moment. It came to me that Mom died the 21st and the day we saw the angel was the 12th. She was also 93 when she died. 9+3=12 and 1+2=3. Both 2+1 and 1+2 add up to 3. It was also three weeks to the day that Mom transitioned. Four sets of numbers surrounding Mom's death all added up to the number 3, which represents the trinity! There are messages in numbers.

Several months after Mom transitioned, I was at my Mentors group five-day weekend where we had begun studying "The Tarot as a Path to Self-Discovery and Spiritual Development." We were using the Rider-Waite deck originally published in 1910. Each card incorporates numerology, esoteric knowledge, the elements in nature (fire, water, earth, air), and what were believed to be powerful astrological events and symbols, most of which are still popular today. I decided to look at the major arcana cards to see how the messages of the cards corresponded to the numbers surrounding Mom's transition.

Mom died the 13th day after having no food or water. The 13th card in the "Rider-Waite" deck is the Death card that symbolizes transformative powers. The meaning of the card is that life has cycles—new life follows when a cycle ends and in between the old and the new lays the natural process of mourning. Mom died on the 21st of September. Card #21 is the World, which represents completion, balance, and support. The symbols on the 21st card indicate that one has been guided to the successful conclusion of their journey. They are whole, renewed, and ready to begin at an even higher level of consciousness. Then I chose to look at the significance of the number three Tarot card, The Empress (Mind, Body, Spirit). The symbology on the card represents the strong feminine energy at work in one's life—nurturing, creativity, and healing. Was it coincidence or synchronicity that the messages on each card aligned with the numbers surrounding Mom's death? It's not surprising to me that the divine energy field would give these messages about transition and love. Looking at the Tarot cards was another beautiful affirmation that Mom's transition happened all in divine order.

> Between the people of eternity and the people of the earth there is constant communication. (Kahlil Gibran)

Witnessing the Love of Sacred Transition

Lucy Lucia

"Offer Julie's mom a healing session. Assist her with her transition," whispered the clear guidance I had come to trust during my morning meditations. With Julie's permission, I prepared to visit Mary. I realized I had never been to a hospice unit before. My sole personal experience with death came over 20 years earlier when my beloved grandmother lay in her busy, crowded, noisy post-surgical hospital room dying from a cancer which had out paced the scalpels. Despite the 24 hour vigil our family kept over the several days preceding her death, she chose to die in the company of a stranger, albeit a compassionate evening nurse, during a brief 15 minute period of time when all family members somehow managed to be absent from her room. I never quite forgave her for that.

As I entered the hospital, I had no idea what to expect. For the past five years I had extensively studied various esoteric fields of subtle energy work. I wondered how my heightened sensitivity to energy would affect me now as I walked among those in transition. As an empath, would I feel the emotional and physical pain and fear of the souls preparing to depart? Or would I feel the grief of the friends and family who would be left behind? I contemplated this and more as I said a prayer to release the quiet and unexpected anxiety that had begun to build somewhere deep within me.

The loud ding of the elevator bell quickly refocused my attention to the reason I was here. I passed a deserted nurses station on my way to Mary's room. This medical unit was eerily silent. I found her room, not far from the elevators. The door was closed. I instinctively knew there was another world behind it, in part, because I knew Julie. I knocked softly and heard my friend gently and softly say, "Come in."

I took a deep breath and carefully pushed the door open. All my senses were instantly engaged as I crossed the threshold of the room and stepped into a much higher vibrational dimension. My first thought/sensation was that this is how church is supposed to feel! This space was peaceful, protected, safe, loving, nurturing, energetically clean and physically uncluttered. It was sacred! It was healing. I could feel my anxiety slip away. The frenzy of the outside world and my imposing and impossible "to do list" no longer existed in this vibration. The energy of the space simply wouldn't allow it. In this special hospital room, we only lived in present time.

It took me a moment to get my bearings because the feel of this space was so exceptionally and dramatically different from the energy back in the quiet hallway. The contrast was breathtaking. Gone was the glaring overhead florescent lighting. In its place was the soft and cozy glow of two bedside table lamps, and natural sunlight filtered in between the blinds on the window. The room smelled heavenly. Literally. I noticed a small essential oil vaporizer on a corner table offering periodic puffs of fragrance. Hmmm, frankincense, I smiled to myself in amusement as I began to understand all my church references. How lovely! No smell of death here.

A beautiful and inspirational version of Ave Maria was softly playing in the background. This peaceful music was the only sound in the room, and we were enveloped in it completely. In some odd way, I instinctively knew the music was instrumental (pun intended) in holding this sacred "container" of energy intact and together. As I walked closer to the bed, I saw Mary, small and frail, lying on her back in deep sleep. She had such a tiny body for such a big soul. She was positioned with multiple blankets cradling her arms and legs. She seemed peaceful, even blissful, and so loved.

Julie was sitting in the corner chair close to her mother's head. She rose to greet me. During our hug I could feel her sadness and her peace. She had maintained a constant vigil for her mom for almost two weeks. Through our phone conversations I was aware of all the internal and energy work she was doing on herself, her mother and her extended family. I understood and appreciated that through this work she was healing her family's lineage forward and back in time.

We spoke in hushed tones in respect for Mary's process. It was a privilege to offer energy work in such a beautifully prepared space. It was joyful to co-create this healing with Julie for her mother. I knew this room would be imprinted with all the wonderful energy and love which flowed through it all these days leading up to Mary's death, and that afterwards, those who found themselves in this room would benefit from it in ways their rational minds would never understand.

I regretted having to leave this wonderful space. As I shut the door to Mary's room behind me and re-entered the third dimensional world, I gave myself permission to forgive my grandmother her chosen method of transition. And I forgave myself for not forgiving her all these years. I swear I could feel her energy smiling down upon me.

PART 2

A HANDBOOK FOR FAMILY, FRIENDS AND CAREGIVERS

CHAPTER 10
Deathbed Promises and Books to Help Prepare You for the Death and Dying Experience

Deathbed Promises

I feel good that I kept the deathbed promise to my father about caring for my mother. There were occasions during the care of mom when I wondered about the ethics surrounding deathbed promises. Deathbed promises are not to be made lightly. My thoughts here are meant to help you reflect on being conscious about making deathbed promises.

Deathbed promises made consciously, openly and freely on the sole initiative of a dying individual's loved one or friend are true commitments. If someone makes a reasonable deathbed promise to a dying friend or loved one, they should make it in good faith and with the intention of fulfilling it. However, if conditions change later making a promise impractical, or the person who made the promise finds him/herself feeling like a victim, rescuer or persecutor (the Victim Triangle) as a result of trying to fulfill the commitment, then having a silent conversation with the person who has transitioned to let them know that the deathbed promise needs to be released into the light is reasonable, fair and ethical. A release ritual as described below may be done.

On the other hand, deathbed promises coerced by a dying friend or relative and made out of kindness or guilt should be re-evaluated at a less emotionally charged time. Again, if the promise is impractical or not conducive to the physical, emotional, psychological or spiritual well-being of the living, then creating a ritual such as writing the promise on a piece of paper, burning it outside and watching the smoke rise while intentionally sending it back to the deceased to gently release it, is in the best interest of all.

Books to Help Prepare You for the Death and Dying Experience

I encourage people of all faiths and cultures and all those working in health care to read about near death and pre-death experiences. It is important to expand our awareness so that we are able to honor and be truly present with our loved ones, friends, clients, and patients as they enter their death and dying experiences. It is also important to prepare ourselves for our own journey into the Light.

Should you choose to read more about pre-death experiences or deathbed visions (DBV), several wonderful books are listed below among books about dying consciously. There are more books listed in the Bibliography.

Anderson, M. (2003). Sacred dying: Creating rituals for embracing the end of life. New York: Marlow and Company Publishers.

Atwater, P. M. H. (2007). The big book of near death experiences: The ultimate guide to what happens when we die. Charlottesville, VA: Hampton Roads Publishing Company, Inc.

Experiencing the soul: Before birth, during life, after death. (2005). Hosted by Eliot Jay Rosen. DVD.

Kelly, P. & Callanan, M. (1997). Final gifts: Understanding the special awareness, needs, and communications of the dying. New York: Bantam Books.

Lerma, J. (2007). Into the light: Real life stories about angelic visits, visions of the afterlife, and other pre-death experiences. Franklin Lakes, NJ: New Page Books. The stories in this book are incredibly touching. Dr. Lerma's compassion and openness to hearing and honoring his dying patients' experiences is truly an inspiration.

Lerma, J. (2009). Learning from the light: Pre-death experiences, prophecies, and angelic messages of hope. Franklin Lakes, NJ: New Page Books. Dr. Lerma shares more angelic messages and mystical experiences given to his patients and their families.

Levine, S. & O. (1982). Who dies?: An investigation of conscious living and conscious dying. New York City: Anchor Books.

Malkin, G. (2003). Unspeakable grace: The music of Graceful Passages. Novato, CA: Wisdom of the World.

Moody, R. (2001). Life after life: The investigation of a phenomenon – survival of bodily death. San Francisco: Harper Collins.

Moyers, B. (2005). On our own terms: Moyers on dying. (Four part series on DVD: Living with Dying, A Different Kind of Care, A Death of One's Own, A Time to Change.) Princeton NJ: Films for the Humanities & Sciences.

Parnia, S. (2006). What happens when we die: A groundbreaking study into the nature of Life and death. Carlsbad, CA: Hay House, Inc.

Singh, K. (1998). Grace in dying: How we are transformed spiritually as we die. New York, NY: HarperCollins Publishers Inc.

Stillwater, M. & Malkin, G. (2003). Graceful passages: A companion for living and dying. (A book and music CD set.) Novato, CA: New World Library.

Willis-Brandon, C. (2000). One last hug before I go: The mystery and meaning of deathbed visions. Deerfield Beach, FL: Health Communications, Inc.

Some interesting web sites (as of 8.02.2011) on which to explore information about death and dying, near-death experiences and deathbed visions are:

www.care-givers.com/DBArticles/pages/viewarticle.php?id=138
www.companionarts.org. Companion Arts is a nonprofit organization utilizing the arts to provide compassionate care, inspiration, and education for people facing the emotional and spiritual challenges of transition and for those who serve them.
www.dyingconsciously.org (Information on Dying Consciously: The Greatest Journey through shamanic traditions.
www.iands.org (International Association for Near-Death Studies)
www.near-death.com (near-death experiences and the afterlife)
www.nderf.org (Near Death Experience Research Foundation)
www.thetwilightbrigade.com. "The sole purpose of Twilight Brigade's bedside volunteers is to provide comfort, reassurance, and compassionate support to the dying and their loved ones. The Twilight Brigade has assisted and comforted thousands of individuals during their final days and hours of life. We have received numerous awards from the highest levels of the Veteran's & Armed Forces' administrations, as well as from U.S. Presidents, for our work in assuring that all our veterans are allowed to die in peace and with dignity. Trained volunteers provide Service at no cost to the patient and/or family!"

CHAPTER 11

Intention, "The Five Wishes," and Life Review

Intention

My use of the word *intention* is based in the definitions of the word by Wayne Dyer in <u>The Power of Intention</u> and by Esther and Jerry Hicks in <u>The Amazing Power of Deliberate Intent</u>. Both books authors write that intention exists in the universe as an invisible field of pure, un-bounding energy that vibrates so fast it defies measurement and observation. One might call it spirit, soul, consciousness, universal mind or source. It is the invisible force that intends everything into the universe. It's everywhere. This source is always creating, it is kind, loving, peaceful, non-judgmental, and it excludes no one.

I see *intention* as consciously choosing what I want to focus on in my life right here, right now. There are two simple rules to creating an intention. The first is to focus on what you want or choose, rather than what you don't want, because what you focus on grows. So the intention needs to be stated positively. The second rule is to state your intention as if you are experiencing it now. So you'd state it in present tense or "I am _____." A couple examples might be "I am confident and feeling successful" or "I am happy and feeling peaceful." To help strengthen manifesting the intention, it's important to imagine, visualize or even do a contemplative meditation that you are already living this intention—seeing it, hearing it and feeling it now, in the present.

You might try creating your own intention and imagine seeing, feeling, and hearing yourself in this state of being, knowing that it's your nature to be living your life this way. One method of doing this is to write your intention on a piece of paper, maybe something like, "I am confident and successful." Write the intention and then write three or four questions about the intention. Several examples are: What does my body posture look like when I am feeling confident and successful? What does my voice sound like when I am confident and successful? How do others perceive me when I am confident and successful? What thoughts do I have when I am confident and successful? Read these questions to yourself several times. Then close your eyes, take a couple of deep breaths to relax and imagine, sense and/or feel yourself being confident and successful.

My intention that I envisioned for Mom was, "The Divine and I are co-creating a peaceful, harmonious transition into the Light for Mom and we are doing so with grace and ease."

Discussing Final Desires and the "Five Wishes"

I encourage readers to talk with their loved ones, clients, or patients about their last desires while they have the physical, emotional, and mental ability to do so. It truly is a gift to the family, when the time comes, to know exactly what someone wants.

There is a wonderful document called "Five Wishes" that gives people a way to control their care and treatment if they become seriously ill and are unable to make their choices known. It is the first advanced medical directive that talks about your personal, emotional and spiritual needs as well as your medical wishes. It meets 42 states' legal requirements for end-of-life care. The five wishes are for:

> The person I want to make care decisions for me when I can't.
> The kind of medical treatment I want or don't want.
> How comfortable I want to be.
> How I want people to treat me.
> What I want my loved ones to know.

I highly recommend everyone 18 years and older think about and complete the "Five Wishes" for themselves. Your local hospice organization may have copies. Information about the document can be found on www.agingwithdignity.org or call (888) 594-7437.

Life Review

The concept of the life review as a developmental task of older adults is defined by Robert Butler (1963) as:

> A naturally occurring, universal mental process characterized by the progressive return to consciousness of past experience, and particularly, the resurgence of unresolved conflicts; simultaneously, and normally, these revived experiences and conflicts can be surveyed and reintegrated . . . prompted by the realization of approaching dissolution and death, and the inability to maintain one's sense of personal invulnerability. (p. 66)

As such it is normal for older adults to consciously or unconsciously look back and reassess their life as they develop a sense of their own mortality and/or in view of imminent death. Butler postulates that the life review offers a final opportunity for the individual to gain some understanding and resolve the conflicts of earlier life. While some people experience the life review process consciously, others tend to experience it in a realm outside of awareness, such as through dreams. Through the experience of the life review process individuals examine whether they feel their life was a success or a failure and what kind of person they have become.

A positive resolution and resultant reorganization of the personality into a more integrated whole allows the individual to be more prepared and accepting of death. However, those individuals who evaluate their lives negatively or as failures often experience physical, emotional, psychological, and spiritual manifestation such as anxiety, anorexia, depression, despair, guilt, and loss of spiritual or religious beliefs thus making the prospect of death difficult to face.

There is also the end-of-life review process that is reported to take place as part of the transition process. Most of the literature on near-death experiences recounts stories of the soul going through a very intensive life review, also called a Recapitulation, as it arrives on the other side. Though this occurs in only minutes of earth time, some people report the life review is very detailed and comprehensive. Most report it as being a positive experience. Raymond Moody, who did extensive studies of near-death experiences, reported that in the cases he studied the judgments came from the individuals themselves and not from the beings of light that seemed to love and accept the people having the near-death experiences. Refer to Chapter 17 for more information.

As health care workers, clergy, and loved ones of those who are elderly or transitioning we have the opportunity to assist with the life review process. The more compassion and forgiveness the dying person can feel for themselves and others, the more peaceful their transition and end-of-life review will be. The following ideas can be especially helpful to those who are struggling:

1. Encourage them to tell you their stories. It might be about their childhood, their career, their happiest memories, or their children. You can audio or video-record their stories. Be a compassionate, non-judgmental listener. (In the case of dementia, Alzheimer's disease or the person being in a coma, tell them the family stories that they told or recount your fondest memories of them.)
2. Help them create a memory book with such items as photographs, memorabilia, or quotes they love.
3. Give them a journal. On top of each page write a question about their life. They can be questions to help them reflect on the past such as "How did Dad propose to you?", "When you were a child, what was your favorite birthday and why?", or "When you were growing up how often did you get together with your cousins?". Or it could be a deeper meaning question such as "How would you like to be remembered?"
4. Have a gathering of loved ones and friends to tell the person how much they have meant to them in their life, acknowledging gifts, kindnesses, and blessings they bestowed on them.
5. Offer to arrange for a clergy person to come to provide spiritual support if it appears that it would be helpful in supporting or resolving issues that come up as part of the life review.
6. Facilitate forgiveness processes when appropriate. What often comes up in the life review process is that there are places the dying person needs to forgive themselves for transgressions. There are two words in forgive ~ give and for. A question that might be asked is "What would

you give for dying in peace and serenity?" A couple of forgiveness processes would be to see what the person is willing to release (give up for) finding the inner peace. One could write what they are willing to release on little pieces of paper and then place them in an appropriate container and do a burning ceremony releasing them to the universe. Another idea is to give the person a flower such as a rose or carnation, as they gently pull off each petal and place it in a small bowl or box, name what they are releasing. The petals can then be taken to a lake, stream, river, etc. and released in the water to be carried away. Doing the burning or petal ceremony naturally depends on logistics. Generally a loved one or caregiver follows through with the ceremony outside of the hospital, nursing home, or hospice environment.

CHAPTER 12

About Vibration, Thoughts and Words

Energetic healer Cyndi Dale states that "Everything in the universe vibrates, and everything that vibrates imparts or impacts information (the definition of energy). Furthermore "Vibrational medicine is the intentional use of a frequency to positively affect another frequency or to bring an organism into balance." Thoughts and words in addition to music, essential oils, and flowers all have the potential to positively affect healing physically, emotionally, psychologically, and spiritually.

In his book <u>Power vs. Force: The Hidden Determinants of Human Behavior</u>, Dr. David Hawkins states that the overall average (vibrational) level of human consciousness is about 207 on a scale of 1000. When our consciousness falls below 200 at any given moment, we start to lose power and grow weaker and are more prone to being manipulated by our surroundings. So, an elderly person living their last years in fear (a vibration of 100) with pain and depression might attract even lower vibrational emotions such as regret, despair, hopelessness, blame, guilt, evil, or shame during their life review process and not remember their experiences of love, hope, joy, etc. When we connect with the vibration of love at 500, and that of joy at 540, we resonate more with our own Christ consciousness and the love that we are. Peace vibrates at 600 and the level of enlightenment is 700-1000 with Lord Krishna, Lord Buddha, and Lord Jesus Christ having a level of 1000.

These vibrational numbers come from a scale researched and developed by David R. Hawkins, M.D., Ph.D. In his book he describes his research that took place over a twenty-year period during which time he tested thousands of people using a specific kinesiology (muscle testing) technique to calibrate his Map of Consciousness.

To me, the importance of Mom's perspective about purgatory was that if she was fearful that she might go to purgatory and she wasn't going to heaven then the vibration of fear (100) might attract more negative vibrations into her life. The law of vibration is a universal law similar to the law of attraction. Universal laws or the laws of nature are defined as the unwavering, unchanging underlying principles that rule our entire universe. They are the means by which our world continues to exist, thrive, and expand. The laws are interrelated and founded on the understanding that everything in the universe is energy and that energy moves in a circular motion. The law of vibration could also be called the law of energy. Quantum physics teaches that no matter how stationary an object may appear, at the molecular level it is in motion. Everything causes vibration. In fact everything we think, feel or say has energy and is in motion. The vibration one is attuned to in the moment will cause one to think and act a certain way, as well as determine what one attracts to oneself. In his book <u>The Divine Matrix</u> Gregg Braden states, "The key to healing is the ability to focus emotion and energy in our bodies or that of a loved one (with the person's permission) in a noninvasive and compassionate way." In other words we can help ourselves and others raise our vibration by using higher vibrational words, thoughts, and emotions.

The concept that thoughts and emotions both spoken and written, and music impact our physical world was also researched by Japanese scientist Dr. Masaru Emoto. Photographs in Dr. Emoto's book The Hidden Messages in Water show that samples of water that were exposed to either positive or negative words, emotions, or thoughts and rock or classical music and then subsequently frozen produced varying crystal formations. Beautiful, perfectly formed crystals were created when the water was exposed to positive influences while water exposed to negativity produced ugly, malformed crystals. One of the most beautiful crystals was extracted from a frozen vial on which the words *love and gratitude* had been written.

Dr. Darren R. Weissman, a chiropractor and holistic healer, who was strongly motivated by Dr. Emoto's work, started photographing samples of patients' blood cells before and after doing healing sessions with a holistic system he created that taps into the power of *Infinite Love and Gratitude.* As part of each healing session Dr. Weissman combined the sign language symbol for *I love you* with the spoken words *Infinite Love and Gratitude* and also had the patients speak intentions they had created in their healing session. The "I love you" sign language symbol or mudra is .

In his book The Power of Infinite Love & Gratitude, pages 237 – 246 contain photographs showing the amazing difference and physical healing that occurred in the before and after blood samples from just one session with clients. When one thinks about the world being composed of approximately 70 percent water and the human body, depending on age and size averaging anywhere between 55% to 78% water, it means humans have the power to evoke positive changes in themselves, others, and on a global level just with the power of their thoughts and words. This is important information for us to integrate. We each have the power to assist the healing of our physical bodies and the planet.

I invite you to think or speak out loud the words Infinite Love and Gratitude and give yourself love with the hand symbol (see above) facing your body. Take several nice deep breaths while you are doing so. Notice if you feel a shift in your energy, which indicates a change in your vibration. Giving yourself infinite love and gratitude is as important as giving it to those you are caring for. It truly is a beautiful gift.

CHAPTER 13

Staying Positive in the Face of Alzheimer's Disease, Illness, Pain, Anxiety and Fear

I know first hand that not all those who struggle with Alzheimer's disease become sweet and loving. In fact the reverse can be true. Some people become abusive verbally, emotionally, and physically. This happens not only with those suffering from Alzheimer's disease, but also with those experiencing other diseases, discomfort, pain and fear of dying. Pain and fear can quickly alter the behavior and outlook of those with otherwise loving personalities. For family members and care givers who hear predominately ugly, mean or hateful things from their loved ones or patients as they transition, I encourage you to remember the words of wisdom by don Miguel Ruiz in his book <u>The Four Agreements</u>. The second agreement states, "Don't take anything personally. Nothing others do is because of you. What others say and do is a projection of their own reality, their own dream. When you are immune to the opinions and actions of others, you won't be the victim of needless suffering."

It's also important to remember that what appears to be grouchy, mean, angry, or verbally and emotionally abusive is not the truth of who the person is. Emotional and physical discomfort, be it physical pain, anxiety, fear, depression, or overwhelm triggers the subconscious mind and brings up old core limiting beliefs one has about oneself, and this can set up negative emotions and behaviors. Examples of limiting beliefs might be beliefs that one is not worthy or not deserving to be healthy or comfortable in their body or go to heaven. It's helpful for me in working with those struggling with pain, fear, anxiety, and other stresses to remember that the negative words and behaviors aren't who they really are. These individuals are really pure love. They just don't know it. So coming from a place of love and compassion is very important and always helpful.

There are also a couple of metaphysical tools you can use to help protect yourself from taking on other people's harsh or negative energy. One is a Cocoon Energy Tool and the other is the Rose Energy Tool. All it takes is for you to use your imagination and to trust the power of the energy tool. The first tool, cocoon imagery, is a meditation. You will want to find a quiet spot where you won't be disturbed, and then read the meditation to yourself several times before you do it.

Cocoon Meditation

Be sure you are in a safe, quiet place where you will not be disturbed. Sit in a position where your body is supported. Move your body around until you are comfortable and starting to feel relaxed. Your arms and legs should be uncrossed. Gently close your eyes and begin to relax your breathing. Take a nice deep breath in all the way from your abdomen up into and through your chest. Hold it. Now slowly let it out. Take another nice long, slow breath in, hold it as long as you can, and then ever so slowly release it. As you continue to breath deeply and slowly, feel a wave of relaxation flow from your head down through to your toes. Feeling calm and relaxed, calm and relaxed.

Now on your next breath, imagine yourself breathing directly into the area in the center of your chest that is your heart center. Breathe into your chest and become aware of your heart center. Breathe into your heart. Now breathe in beautiful golden light right into your heart. With each in-spirit-ation and ex-spirit-ation of this golden light you are breathing in your spirit of pure love.

Feel this golden light and pure love now pulsing out from your heart and flowing to each and every cell, organ, and muscle of your body. Your body is healing with each heartbeat and each inhalation and exhalation. You are pure love. Now see, sense, or feel this light flowing out your fingertips, the soles of your feet, the top of your head, and on the wave of your breath. Feel the light spreading around you. Soon you are surrounded with this beautiful golden light that extends at least three feet all around you. It gently and lovingly encloses you in a cocoon of beautiful light. Feel how peaceful, calm and relaxed you are in the center of this cocoon of light.

Now, with whatever color you choose, create a shell of light around the outside of this cocoon, just like an egg has a shell protecting it's soft center. Use your breath to imagine creating this protective shell around your cocoon of beautiful golden light. Notice how safe you feel. You can rest easily inside this cocoon of light.

This shell protects you and holds you in the center of your cocoon of pure love. This shell is semi-permeable. It only allows one thing to pass through it. Only unconditional love can flow through the shell. Pure love freely passes in and out. Now imagine someone you love in front of you. Notice how easily this loves flows from your heart out through the shell to them. Now notice how easily their love comes through the shell to be received by you. Breathe in this love. See, feel or imagine this flow of love going back and forth between you.

Now imagine your loved one or a patient who is abusive emotionally or verbally, someone who has drained your energy in the past sitting across from you. Feel yourself sitting inside your cocoon of golden light surrounded and protected by the shell. From this place of love and protection, see their energy simply bouncing off your shell. It cannot come in. It doesn't matter how much they try, you are centered and relaxed inside your shell. From this place of safety and love, you can choose to respond in a way that best serves the highest good of both of you.

Several times a day, use your breath, the in-spirit-ation and ex-spirit-ation of the golden light of pure love, and see more of your shell color flowing down to strengthen and reinforce its protective power. Set the intention that, "I am always protected in my cocoon, feeling safe and pure love."

Notice how your interactions change and how your energy level stays stronger.

Rose Energy Tool

Roses have been used metaphysically for hundreds of years as a tool to clear energy as they have a very high vibration. Follow the steps below.

1. Imagine or remember what a long stem rose looks like. The rose can be any color.
2. Visualize placing the rose at the edge of your energy field (edge of your cocoon) or half way between you and someone else. Just imagine the rose circulates around the edge of your energy field, around the circumference of your energy field with you in the middle. Set the intention that it will continually strengthen your boundaries.

3. Now imagine someone who drains your energy sitting or standing in front of you. The rose is half way between you and this person. Keep your beautiful, loving peaceful energy focused on your side of the rose, on the distance between you and the rose. When you do, the other person's energy will stay on their side of the rose, in the space between the rose and them.
4. Everything on the other side of the rose, between the rose and the other person is for you to <u>observe</u>, like watching a Shakespeare play. You only observe what the characters on the stage are saying and doing. You don't get involved. Similarly, you allow the other person across from you to be in their energy. With the rose in place you don't take on the other person's energy. The rose takes on and filters out the energy, sending the negative energy down its long stem to be transmuted into helpful fertilizer for Mother Earth. You stay in your calm relaxed place without taking on their energy. This exercise with the rose helps you develop neutrality and compassionate detachment from other people's negative thoughts, words, and actions.
5. Occasionally check in with your rose. Is it becoming discolored? Are the petals drooping or falling off? Thank it for protecting you and gently freshen it up or exchange it for a new one.
6. Again, as with the Cocoon Meditation, notice how your interactions with others change. Observe any shift in your own energy when you use the rose.

Another "tool" would be to embrace your loved one's or patient's reactions to their disease and stress with an attitude of gratitude. What a beautiful lesson, or challenge, they are providing for you to stay in your own loving energy and to practice patience and compassion. You might give them and yourself Infinite Love and Gratitude in your thoughts, words, and/or by using the "I love you" hand mudra 🤟. (Refer back to page 107.)

If you are comfortable with it I also encourage you to take advantage of any counseling opportunities surrounding any physical symptoms and/or feelings of anger, frustration, overwhelm, grief, or loss you might be experiencing. This can be a very stressful time in your life. Whatever you are feeling be it physical or emotional, is a gift, an opportunity for healing and personal growth. You might check to see if your work place has an Employee Assistance Program (EAP) through their Human Relations Department. EAP offers employees the possibility of seeing a social worker or psychotherapist. If your family is using hospice for your loved one, generally there are a social worker and a chaplain on the team who are available to work with the family members. Know that there are supportive services available and take advantage of them.

CHAPTER 14
The Facts About Terminal Dehydration

It might be helpful for the reader to know that evidence indicates that The general impression among hospice clinicians is that starvation and dehydration do not contribute to suffering among the dying and might actually contribute to a comfortable passage or transition. (Byock, 1995) Dehydration does not cause death, but effectively reduces pain and allows the disease process to take its natural course. Research has shown that with dehydration there are natural endorphins (anesthetics) produced in the brain that help relieve pain and can help reduce the amount of pain medication needed at the end of life. In patients with heart failure, liver and kidney failure giving fluids may actually over hydrate patients and cause them to drown in their own secretions. (Retrieved 4.24.2011 from www.hospicecareflorida.org/care-grief.php)

Death by terminal dehydration is not painful and the attendant physical discomfort such as parched, cracked lips, a swollen tongue, dry skin, or higher body temperatures can be adequately alleviated by palliative care. It typically takes several days to two or three weeks for death to occur by this means, and the time involved depends on the state of hydration in which the patient enters the process. While the vigils of family members awaiting their loved one's death by this process may seem long and stressful, concerned relatives and friends need to understand that offering the patient minimal drinking in response to thirst or physical discomfort may further prolong the process of dying. Anecdotal evidence suggests that terminal dehydration can provide a peaceful and dignified process of dying. (Miller & Meier, 1998)

CHAPTER 15

Tools to Clear Space at Home or in a Health Care Setting

In Dr. Lerma's book <u>Into the Light,</u> he writes about how the staff on the hospice unit where he worked experienced different energies in the patients' rooms, even after patients had died and were no longer in the rooms:

> Nurses report that certain rooms have specific energies and repeatedly attract the same kind of patient. Could it be that these rooms hold a specific type of electromagnetic energy? The hospice staff frequently hears eerie noises in certain rooms, such as deep, synchronous breathing (similar to that of a ventilator), even when no machine or patient is in the room. In other rooms, one might hear laughing or the sound of animals. It's as if the room is assigned to a particular experience and that it holds doorways to different dimensions with varying entities to help one with their life review. (p. 109)
>
> Jan and the chaplain stated that, as he exhaled his last breath, a white flash emanated from his chest and flew out the window. Several hours after this people who walked into his room were able to experience the remnant static energy. (p. 184)

The following tools may be used to clear the patient's room before, during, or after they occupy the room.

Creating an Energy Vortex

1. Draw lines into the center of the room from the four corners of the ceiling and the floor. Where these eight lines meet, a vortex is created.
2. Visualize or imagine a whirling or spiraling column of energy moving counter clockwise sending or releasing all negative energy down into the ground or out the window into the universe.
3. Invoke that any intentional or unintentional non-virtuous energy that anyone brings into the room by thought, word, behavior, etc. will immediately go out the vortex and be transmuted by the Violet Flame of St. Germaine to healing, transforming virtuous energy to be used by Mother Earth.
4. Invoke that this vortex will remain in place until you remove it.

Prayer

As mentioned previously, an effective way to raise one's vibration or the vibration of a room is through prayer and this can be done by intentionally sending prayer through time and space. In his book <u>The Divine Matrix</u> and his CD course <u>Speaking the Lost Language of God</u>, Gregg Braden cites numerous modern scientific studies, research, and experiments that prove what the ancients of all faith traditions and indigenous peoples had been saying since the beginning of time is correct. There is an unseen web of intelligent energy that connects everything. Some call it the Mind of God and others call it The Divine Matrix. Quantum physicists call it the quantum hologram. Braden writes, "The Divine Matrix is the *container* that holds the universe, the *bridge* between all things, and the *mirror* that shows us what we have created." This web of energy contains all our thoughts, dreams, actions, emotions, and prayers. Braden states, "The universally connected hologram of consciousness promises that the instant we create our good wishes and prayers, they are already received at their destination."

Entrainment or Coherency

In many of his workshops and books Gregg Braden also teaches about coherency or entrainment. In physics entrainment is defined as the energetic interlocking of two rhythms that have similar frequencies. I mentioned when sitting with Mom I would quiet my mind and hold the vibration of love, compassion, appreciation, forgiveness and gratitude in my heart with the intention of having her heart and brain entrain to mine. Research from The Institute of HeartMath (www.heartmath.org) shows that the heart's electromagnetic field, the most powerful electromagnetic field produced by the body, envelopes every cell of the body & extends out in all directions into the space around us. The heart communicates with the brain electromagnetically, neurologically, biophysically, and biochemically. As people learn to sustain heart-focused positive feeling states (happiness, compassion, love, joy), the brain can be brought into entrainment with the heart.

The Institute of HeartMath has scientific instruments that are able to measure that with entrainment, one vibration actually moves a second one out of its resonant frequency. When people touch or are in proximity, one person's heartbeat signal is registered in the other person's brainwaves. This energy exchange between individuals is central to healing techniques. Thus as loved ones or care givers we can lower or raise the vibration of the one for whom we are caring. Coherency describes a positive entrainment, intentionally creating a heart connection with the purpose of raising the vibration of the other person.

A wonderful resource for information and meditations regarding coherency is the Global Coherence Initiative (GCI), a science based, co-creative project to unite people in creating planetary peace. The web site is www.glcoherence.org.

Music

I have found in my hospice volunteer work that people with dementia and/or those who are transitioning and receiving pain medication often experience having the television on in their rooms creates visual and auditory confusion. They often think there is a stranger or two in their room. My personal experience is that once the television is off the energy and confusion in the room changes, so when I volunteer on the hospice In-Patient Unit I ask permission to turn the television off and put on some soothing music. When I play a CD of gentle harp music or other music designed to induce peace and calm in the room the patient's breathing pattern shifts and they become more relaxed. There are many excellent music CD's available for inducing a calm and peaceful state and raising the vibration in the room. If you want to listen to the music before you buy it, you can go to iTunes.com or amazon.com and search "relaxation music" or "inner peace music." Albums from various artists will come up and you can often listen to 20-30 seconds of different tracks to see if you like the track or album before you purchase it.

Violet Flame

The Violet Flame is a metaphysical or spiritual tool used since ancient times to transmute negative energy into positive energy. The color violet has been associated with spirituality for centuries. It has the highest frequency in the visible colors on the spectrum of light. Metaphysicians teach that this fundamentally transformative, transcendent and uplifting spiritual energy accelerates life at the etheric, mental, emotional and physical levels.

Positive and Negative Energy

While I don't like using terms such as good/bad, light/heavy, and negative/positive, we live in a world of contrasts. It is easier to explain the differences in how energy feels by using these contrasting words. The terms negative and positive energy refer to how we personalize energy in and around us. We each feel and express emotions that cause us to feel good (positive) or bad (negative). Some might express it as feeling lighter or heavier energetically. For example a person exhibiting positive energy may elicit within you feelings of peace, safety, and relaxation and you enjoy being in their presence. The love, compassion and support you feel attract you to this person, and you feel good/lighter when you are around them. On the other hand, a person exhibiting negative energy may leave you with a sense of being devalued, and attacked, and you likely feel tense and unsafe in their presence. Their off-putting, uncomfortable vibes may make you want to get away from them. You may even feel cranky, tired, ill, or like your energy is heavier after being around some people. The medical field is now beginning to recognize that the attitude of the patient has a very large impact on how fast that patient's healing progresses. Therefore helping patients achieve a positive state can promote healing. In the sacred setting of preparing for transitioning, it is important to maintain an energy of love, compassion, peace, and forgiveness to help the dying person continue to heal spiritually to make their transition.

Essential Oils

Essential oils distilled from plants have been used for physical and spiritual healing for centuries, in many cultures and religions. Many references to anointing and healing with oils can be found in the Bible. What is most important in choosing an oil is the energy of the essential oil, its vibrational quality or frequency.[10] Measurements of healthy human bodies found they resonate at an energetic frequency around 62-68 megahertz (MHz). Essential oils range in frequency between 52-320 MHz, the highest of all known substances.[11] In addition, it has been shown that applying essential oils in an attitude of prayer enhances their effectiveness.

When using essential oils, look for and purchase only oils labeled therapeutic grade in order to ensure that you get oils with the highest vibration. The high vibration of many of these oils wards off the bombardment of negative energy and increases the individual's sense of balance, harmony, peace and gentleness, thus relieving nervous tension and stress. Some protective oils are White Angelica™, sandalwood, Peace and Calming®, frankincense, rose, and geranium. In J. Stone's book <u>The Complete Ascension Manual</u>, he states, "The scent of sandalwood has the metaphysical effect of breaking down the old energies. This quality of energy is exactly what is needed at the time of death."

A couple of web sites that sell therapeutic grade oils are: <u>www.youngliving.com</u>, <u>www.rockymountainoils.com</u> and <u>http://auroma.com</u>. It is important to note that essential oils are very concentrated and are not intended to be applied directly to the skin unless diluted in a carrier oil such as jojoba oil or olive oil. Some essential oils already come in carrier oils. Essential oils may be used full strength for aromatherapy purposes.

---

[10] Worwood, 1999
[11] Stewart, 2010

Always read the label to determine if the essential oil has been approved for ingestion, skin contact and/or aromatherapy.

When using essential oils to anoint someone or to infuse their or your own aura, place two to three drops of the oil in the palm of your hand. Make several clockwise circles in the oil with your fingers from the opposite hand. Then rub your palms together. For yourself, cup your palms over your nose and deeply inhale the aroma invoking that you be a channel of God's light and love. To anoint another, you can make the Sign of the Cross on the forehead while saying a prayer or you may choose to bless or anoint the person with a special prayer over each of their seven major chakras while you rotate your essential oil infused palms in a clockwise direction three times over each chakra. Using essential oils is healing for both you, your loved one, or patient.

Using a Pendulum to Help Decision-Making

Intuition is receiving input and ideas without knowing exactly how and where they come from. It often feels as if it is not from oneself. Some people describe it as having a gut feeling, a knowing, sixth sense, inner sense, instinct, inner voice, spiritual guidance, etc. Intuitive decision-making usually involves accessing unconscious or subconscious senses to perceive and translate information from outside oneself. For those who may not yet trust their intuition in selecting essential oils, music, or flowers, the use of a pendulum may be helpful. A pendulum is simply a small weighted, symmetrical object hanging on a chain or string so that it swings freely under the influence of gravity. The object can be metal, crystal, glass, or wood. Smaller lightweight pendulums are easier and quicker to use and chains or strings that hang no more than three inches respond faster than those on a longer chain or string.

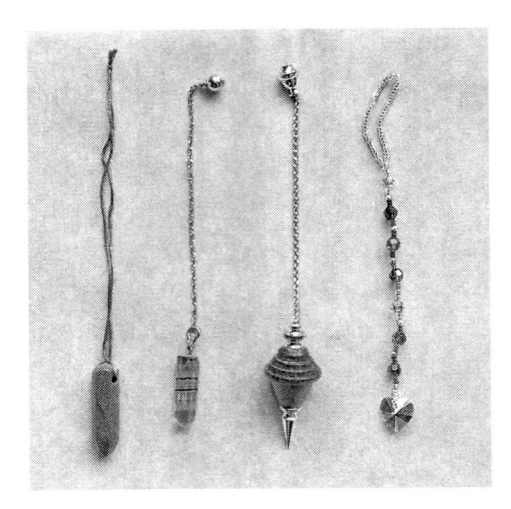

Using a pendulum is like a form of muscle testing called kinesiology. The subtle energy around your physical body responds to your subconscious, thoughts, and words to move the pendulum and answer your questions. Your subtle energy bodies may hold answers to the questions you ask or they may be the intermediary between you and your higher self, soul and spirit guides, as well as the souls of other people. Thus you can use the pendulum to ask yes and no questions to make decisions about which essential oils, music, or flowers are the best to use to help raise the vibration of your loved one, client, or patient when they are not able to verbally communicate their wishes to you. Using the pendulum in this manner is called dowsing.

It is very important to be grounded to connect your energy field to the healing properties of Mother Earth and pull in your soul and higher aspects for guidance before you start using your pendulum. Grounding yourself before you make contact with your subtle energy bodies and spiritual guides is a simple but important process. Here is a suggested step-by-step approach to grounding and then using a pendulum:

1. Take a couple of nice deep abdominal breaths to relax and quiet your mind.
2. Imagine tree roots growing down from the soles of each foot rooting you firmly into the center of Mother Earth. If tree roots don't resonate with you try visualizing a tube, cord or any other connecting device that feels comfortable to you.
3. Connect to your Higher Self through your crown chakra by visualizing a bright golden white star ten inches above your head and draw a strand of the golden white light from the star down through your crown chakra (the top of your head) and into your heart chakra.
4. Center your energy by focusing on your heart center. Feel it expanding until it becomes the source from which you operate, rather than the conscious mind.
5. Intend that only healing, transforming energy flow through you and around you during this process.
6. Take your pendulum and hold the string or chain gently between your thumb and forefinger. Hold it so that the pendulum weight dangles 2 to 3 inches from where you've grasped it. The length will determine how fast it will swing. The shorter the length of chain or string the faster the pendulum will swing.
7. Let your pendulum dangle and swing gently in a neutral fashion. Keep your hand and arm relaxed. Tensing up will prevent the pendulum from swinging freely.
8. Ask your spiritual guides to show you a 'yes' and see how the pendulum swings. In my case a yes swings in a clockwise circle. Then ask your spiritual guides to show you a 'no' and see how the pendulum swings. For some people it may be counterclockwise, while for others it may simply swing back and forth. Then test your pendulum by asking a question in your mind for

which you know the answer is a 'yes'. I might ask, "Is my name Julie?" Then ask a question in your mind for which the answer is a 'no'. I usually ask if I'm an age that is older than I really am.

9. Continue to ask questions for which you know the answers until you are confident how the pendulum will swing to indicate a 'yes' response and how it will swing to indicate 'no'.
10. Once you have established your 'yes' and 'no' swings you can start to ask other questions that require a yes or no answer. Let's say you want to know if your loved one (who is unable to physically communicate with you) would like to listen to some spiritual music that s/he has enjoyed in the past. Ask your spiritual guides and your loved one's higher self for the correct answers. It is important to ask that the answer be for the higher good of your loved one. Be sure to ask only one yes/no question at a time.

The questions might go:

Question	Answer
Does _____ want to listen to Panis Angelicus?	No
Does _____ want to listen to Ave Maria?	Yes
Does s/he want an Ave Maria by Shubert?	No
Does s/he want an Ave Maria by Gounod?	Yes
Does s/he want an instrumental version?	Yes

This same technique may be used for determining what prayers your loved one might like said out loud or what essential oils or flowers they would like to have in the room. There are also a couple of other ways to use the pendulum. For example, if you have bottles of essential oil, you can set them on a table a couple inches apart from each other. Place the pendulum over each bottle and ask if your loved one would like you to diffuse that oil or anoint them with that oil. See if the pendulum gives you a yes or no. Another technique would be to write the name of one essential oil or one type of flower such as daisy, rose, or lilac on separate pieces of paper, one oil or flower per piece of paper. Then holding the pendulum over the paper ask if your loved one would like that flower in the room or that essential oil to be diffused.

CHAPTER 16

Cleansing and Illuminating All Seven Chakras

The Incas teach that the newborn's chakras are each bright, glowing and spinning at the optimum vibration. As we grow older the color in our chakras becomes dull. The trauma and loss in our lives leave toxic residues or heavy, lower vibrational energies (sludge) behind in each chakra. The sludge that adheres to the chakras does not permit them to vibrate at their pure frequency. This prohibits the soul from taking spirit flight. When the chakras are cleared and illuminated, they spin freely and vibrate with their original purity again. The Amazon shamans believe that when all the chakras are clear, you acquire a "rainbow body" that allows the soul to take Spirit flight through the crown chakra into the Light or Spirit world.

Exercise:

1. Ask permission of person.
2. Set intention that heavy energies be cleared from each chakra for highest good of person (or animal).
3. Open Eighth Chakra to connect with Divine, feel heart expand with Light and positive feelings.

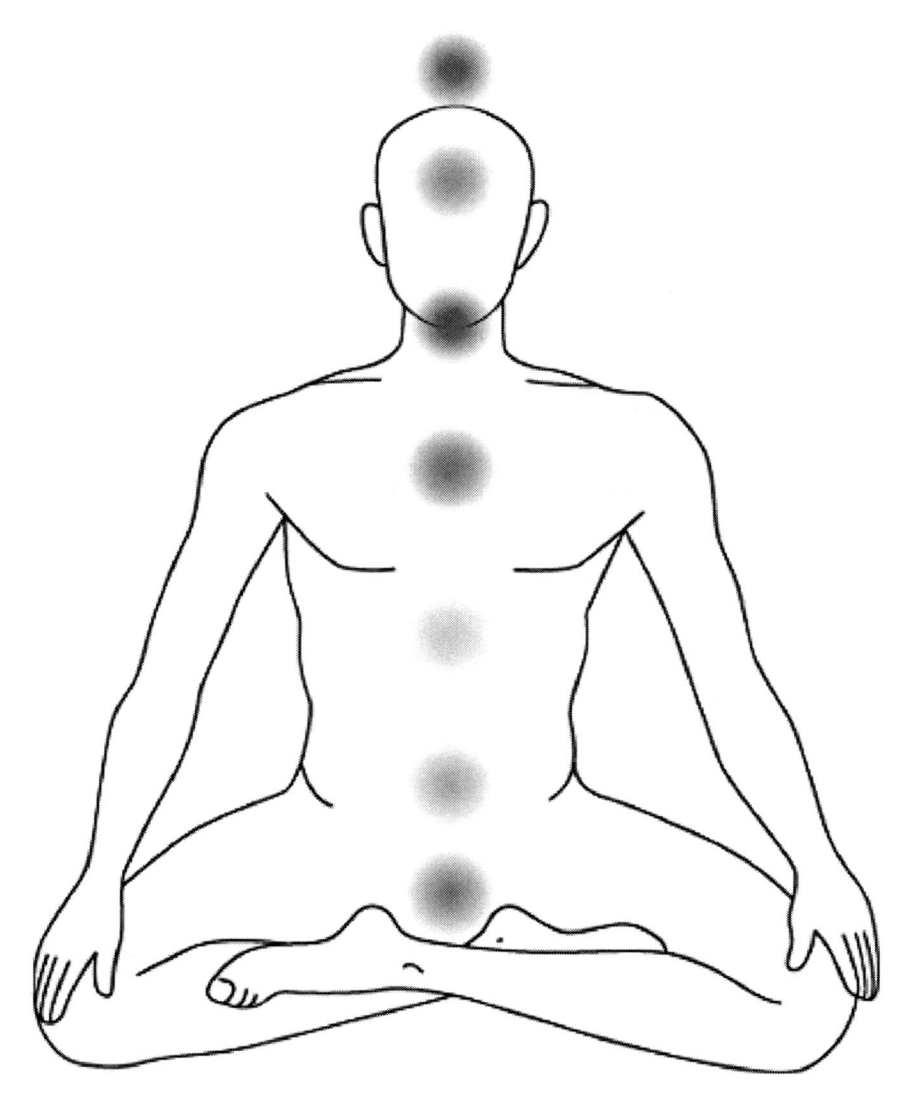

4. Procedure for working with each chakra starting with the 1st (root) and moving up to the 7th (crown)
   a. Place your hand over the chakra about 2" - 3" away from the body.
   b. Open the chakra by slowly spinning your hand in a counterclockwise direction 5-10 times.

- c. See, sense, or feel (or use the power of intention) the heavy energy in the chakra vortex, remove it, and release it to Mother earth to be fertilizer.
- d. Illuminate the chakra with Divine healing light. You may sense its color getting more vibrant.
- e. Close the chakra by slowly spinning your hand clockwise 5-10 times.

5. Follow this procedure for all seven chakras
   1st chakra (red, root) at pelvic bone
   2nd chakra (orange, sacral) 2-3 fingers below the navel
   3rd chakra (yellow, solar plexus) solar plexus
   4th chakra (green, heart) center of the chest
   5th chakra (blue, throat), hollow of the throat
   6th chakra (indigo, third eye), middle of the forehead
   7th chakra (violet, crown) very top of the head
6. Give thanks to your spiritual guides for being with you.
7. Close the Eighth Chakra

CHAPTER 17
Self Care for the Caretakers

It is very important for medical and spiritual healers, family members and friends who are helping loved ones transition to stay connected to Source (God, Divinity, Universal Oneness, whatever that is for you) and their spiritual guides, to stay in the flow of receiving divine information, and to give themselves the time and space to integrate all that is happening. It is important to stay grounded or in one's body in order to be present, conscious and aware of this sacred experience and to be able to integrate and remember it.

Daily prayers, invocations, meditation, or breath work, are ways to stay connected to the Divine. Consider using this Invocation for yourself for protection, healing, love and guidance:

> Divine Mother-Father God, Infinite Love and Wisdom, all the angels and archangels, and all my spiritual guides I invoke your divine healing, love, protection, guidance, and presence on all levels of my being - physically, mentally, emotionally, spiritually – past, present, future and parallel lives. Place your shield of protection in and around me and protect me from all negative energy (throughout my day or as I lay down to rest).

I request that your sacred/divine shield continues to protect me (during the day or my sleep time) so that I may utilize this time to directly connect myself with your divine healing, guidance and love. Protect me during any astral travels so that I may be a source of love, healing and service to every living system I meet. Protect my soul so it comes back whole, filled with only divine love and wisdom.

Transform my cells, organs, and physiological systems to healthier and youthful ones. Transform all my thoughts to healthy, loving thoughts filled with wisdom. I invoke that only divine white light lives in me and around me at all times. So be it now. And so it is. Thank you. Amen.

Using a grounding cord is a spiritual or metaphysical tool to help you be grounded, and to release negative thoughts & emotions through and to bring up healing energy from Mother Earth. Here is a more thorough technique for creating a grounding cord than was described when working with a pendulum:

1. Find a quiet place where you will not be disturbed.
2. Begin with <u>Energy breathing</u> - deep, circular abdominal breathing to slow down all the physical, emotional and mental body systems to induce a state of calmness.
3. Bring your attention to the base of your spine, to your tailbone. Use your imagination to create a cord (a rope, tree trunk, cable, whatever you want) from the tip of your tailbone all the way down to the center or core of Mother Earth.
4. See, sense or feel the grounding cord firmly in place on both ends. For example, if it's a tree trunk you might envision a strong root system. Take another deep, slow

circular breath and sense yourself feeling stronger, more solid, and perhaps even taller.
5. Now in your minds eye, expand the grounding cord to a diameter of about 6".
6. See, sense or feel a golden star about 10" above the top of your head. This solar star holds universal light and love. See, sense, imagine, or feel beautiful golden light coming from the star down through the top of you head (crown chakra) and traveling down through all your spinal column, all your chakras pulling into it all the lower vibrational thoughts, emotions, dis-ease, dis-comfort that are yours or that you have taken on from others.
7. Set the intention that all these lower vibrational energies be transmuted by the Violet Flame of St. Germaine into healing energies that Mother Earth may use.
8. See, sense or feel all negative thoughts, emotions, dis-comforts of the day being pushed down through the grounding cord going into Mother Earth.
9. When this feels complete, activate the flow of even more beautiful golden white healing light from the solar star coming into your spinal column and nervous systems healing your physical, emotional, mental and spiritual bodies.
10. Do this exercise at least once a day, especially before you go to bed at night. You can also set the intention that your grounding cord will always be magnetized to pull any negativity from your system.
11. Occasionally, it is a good idea to drop your old grounding cord and establish a new one. Do this by visualizing the old cord dropping down into Mother Earth while at the same time a new grounding cord is coming down from your tailbone area. I like to thank the old grounding cord for its service before I release it.

CHAPTER 18
The End-of-Life Life Review

There are many people who have experienced the life review process as part of their Near Death Experiences (NDEs). Though their experiences may be slightly different, their message is that the life review process is an amazing gift that offers an opportunity for atonement (at one ment) and forgiveness. Some describe it has seeing their life pass before them in a 360° panorama while others describe it as if a film is playing before them, either backwards or forwards.

Consistently it's reported that the review contains all incidents of life that are charged positively and negatively and some report it's not only this life time, but every life time that you have lived. It's an opportunity to review consciously everything that you have done up to that moment and shed the karma from all those lives. It is reported that it's not a day of judgment where you are judged. But instead, you are in the life review process as a dignified human being. You yourself are the judge, jury, defending attorney, and the defendant. People often report after these experiences that they are better able to forgive themselves and others and live each moment of their lives more consciously and fully.

Those who have been through the life review process say they no longer fear death.[12] In the film "Infinity: The Ultimate Trip" Dannion Brinkley says, "There is no death" and Neale Donald Walsch calls it "Our continuation day."[13] It is after all sacred transition, releasing the physical realm to be born again into the spiritual realm.

---

[12] Atwater, 2007, Brinkley, 2008, Weidner, 2008
[13] Weidner, 2008

Afterward

During the first few days of sitting down to write this book, I did a process I learned in a subtle energy course that allows a person to connect with the Higher Self of someone, whether living or dead. The way this works is you write the person's full name on a piece of paper and also write down their birth date if you know it. Have with you either a photograph of the person or something that belonged to them. Find a quiet still place by yourself where you will not be disturbed. Next write out one or more questions you would like to ask the Higher Self of the friend or relative you wish to communicate with. Select one of the questions to ask. After you have done this, hold the piece of paper with their name and the item that belonged to them in your hand and place your hand up to your heart. Have a pad of paper and pen or pencil by you. Close your eyes and visualize the person and ask their Higher Self the question.

Listen with your inner senses for the answer. As soon as you start to receive an answer, open your eyes and write down what comes to you as fast as you can. Don't filter the response or think about it. Just listen and write. You can reflect on the answer later.

I did this exercise with both my parents. Here are my questions and their responses:

Dad, what would you like me to know about the visions you shared with me?

"You did the best you could. We both did. I didn't understand your question about forgiveness. I would have asked for forgiveness for not being a better father, more present, more compassionate. I thought you were asking for forgiveness and I couldn't think of anything you needed forgiveness for.

"Thank you for honoring my visions. Mom was right. Ruth was a cousin. It meant a lot that you said you would care for Mary. I could rest in peace knowing she'd be okay. I released guilt about dying before her."

(I guess Dad had more that he wanted to share than just answer my question.)

Dad, is there any special message you want me to share in the book?

"Please tell people that it's important for family and friends to listen and pay attention to the words of dying loved ones and to honor the visions as they are very real. Also to honor the strength and courage it takes to die, to prepare to leave the physical body and loved ones behind.

"One of our most tender moments was when you got on the mattress that was on the floor and you held me when I was having the seizures from the medication. That meant a lot to me that you weren't afraid to do that. Thank you."

Mom, what do you want me to get across to people in the book?

"The importance of love. You gave me so much unconditional love. It helped me to see myself in a new way. I was love, am love. You filled me with love and light. I saw myself as love and truly lovable for the first time in my life. I felt worthy of God's love. I felt worthy to go to Heaven to be with God in all that love.

"And Julie, you were right. Everyone was there waiting for me, arms outstretched. Everyone was healthy and light and love. I would never have imagined the beauty, the joy, and the celebration of me coming Home, of so many people helping me go Home. And yes, your dad knows how to make lace. Who would have thought it? And Kevin and my mom send their love. They were with us in the room at hospice all the time, along with Aunt Lu and many beautiful angels. You were constantly being supported, as was I.

"There was so much love. It was the love and the constant encouragement to let go of earthly thoughts about myself and to go into the Light and the love. Talk about the power of love, holding no grudges, no fears. It was LOVE. If you can explain about getting to that place of love in your heart, the heart connection with me and God, that will sell the book. That is the key to helping others transition—being in the place of love, being in the place of joy that I was going Home."

Anything else Mom?

"No, just the love, the whole environment of being surrounded by love, peace, and joy."

Thanks Mom. I love you.

"You're welcome. I know you do. I love you too."

Acknowledgments

I wish to express unending gratitude to the many people who have made this book possible. For those family members, friends, students, patients, and clients who have taught me though their sickness, grief, and dying process. I am forever grateful and inspired by you.

To the quantum physicists who have placed the field of metaphysics and parapsychology on firm ground, I am grateful and indebted to you.

I applaud all those who are leading the way in conscious living and dying. You are making a difference for so many individuals and families.

Thank you to all my family and friends for the generous love and support you have provided during the creation of this book.

And a special thanks to Carol Holaday, who worked with the final version of the book bringing it to fruition.

About the Author

Julie M. Milne, PhD is a Licensed Clinical Professional Counselor, health and transpersonal psychotherapist, and clinical hypnotherapist, in addition to being a Reiki Master, Reiki Phowa Practitioner, and Certified Breath Therapist. She holds a Bachelor of Science degree in Metaphysical Healing, a Masters degree in Counseling, a PhD in Health Psychology, and has studied the practice of living and dying consciously since 2002. Julie also is a Certified Instructor of Dying Consciously. Having worked in hospital settings for 15 years, Julie currently maintains a private practice, and facilitates personal transformation workshops. She has presented at local, state and national conferences in the fields of counseling, dietetics, needle arts, and dying consciously and has published articles in national professional journals. Her meditation CDs, <u>Eliciting the Relaxation Response and Inner Peace</u>, <u>Healing Your Shadow Parts</u>, <u>Medicine Wheel Healing Meditation</u>, and <u>Channel of Light: Gong & Guided Imagery Meditation</u> have sold in over twelve countries. Julie lives with her husband, Rich, in Northbrook, Illinois and volunteers her time working with patients in a Chicago area hospice.

Bibliography

Atwater, P.M.H. (2004). We live forever: The real truth about death with wisdom from the Edgar Cayce readings. Virginia Beach, VA: A.R.E. Press.

Atwater, P. M. H. (2007). The big book of near death experiences: The ultimate guide to what happens when we die. Charlottesville, VA: Hampton Roads Publishing Company, Inc.

Braden, G. (2005). Speaking the lost language of God: Awakening the forgotten wisdom of prayer, prophecy and the dead sea scrolls. (CD course) Niles, IL: Nightingale Conant.

Braden, G. (2007). The divine matrix: bridging time, space, miracles, and belief. Carlsbad, CA: Hay House, Inc.

Brinkley, D. (2008). Saved by the light: The true story of a man who died twice and the Profound revelations he received. New York: Harper One.

Butler, R. N. (1963). The life review: An interpretation of reminiscence in the aged. Psychiatry, 26, 65-75.

Chopra, D. (2004). The book of secrets: Unlocking the hidden dimensions of your life. New York: Harmony Books.

Chopra, D. (2008). Life after death: The burden of Proof. New York City: Harmony Books.

Cohen, L. (Narrator). (1994). The Tibetan book of the dead (A way of life: The great liberation. Life after death). Canada:

National Film Board of Canada in cooperation with NHG Japan and Mistral Film of France.

Cope, D. (2008). Dying: A natural passage. Santa Fe: Three Whales Publishing.

Cristman, Y. (2005). The Bardo: The ultimate journey, a contemporary approach. Three-day workshop notebook, Chicago, IL.

Crosby, G. & D. Culley. (2003). Anesthesia, the aging brain, and the surgical patient. Canadian Journal of Anesthesia 50:R12. Retrieved from http://springerlink.com/content/735243g150171435/fulltext.pdf

Dale, C. (2009). The subtle body: An encyclopedia of your energetic anatomy. Boulder, CO: Sounds True.

DeSpelder, L. & A. Strickland. (1999). The last dance: Encountering death and dying. Mountain View, CA: Mayfield Publishing Company.

Dyer, W. (2004). The power of intention: Learning to co-create your world your way. Carlsbad, CA: Hay House, Inc.

Emoto, M. & D. Thayne. (2004). The hidden messages in water. Hillsboro, OR: Beyond Words Publishing.

Experiencing The Soul: The Video. This inspiring video explores five major categories of soul-experiences, the spiritual aspects of the death-process, supportive scientific evidence, and how to contact our soul-essence in everyday life. To order, call 1-877-965-1279 or email at eliotrosen@hotmail.com.

Filippi, G. (1996). MRTYU: Concept of death in Indian traditions. New Delhi: D.K. Printworld (P) Ltd.

Ghimire (Poudyal), G. & B. Ghimire. (1998). Hindu death rites (Antyeshti Samskar). Napal: Napal Lithographing Co. Pvt. Ltd.

Halifax, J. (2009). Being with the dying: Cultivating compassion and fearlessness in the presence of death. Boston: Shambhala Publications, Inc.

Hawkins, D. (2002). Power vs. Force: The hidden determinants of human behavior. Carlsbad, CA: Hay House, Inc.

Hay, L. (1999). You can heal your life. Carlsbad, CA: Hay House, Inc.

Hicks, E. & Hicks, J. (2006). The amazing power of deliberate intent: Living the art of allowing. Carlsbad, CA: Hay House, Inc.

Kubler-Ross, E. (1991). On life after death. Berkeley, CA: Celestial Arts.

Lerma, J. (2007). Into the light: Real life stories about angelic visits, visions of the afterlife, and other pre-death experiences. Franklin Lakes, NJ: New Page Books.

Lerma, J. (2009). Learning from the light: Pre-death experiences, prophecies, and angelic messages of hope. Franklin Lakes, NJ: New Page Books.

Levine, S. & O. (1982). Who dies?: An investigation of conscious living and conscious dying. New York City: Anchor Books.

Lewis, M, I. Nevo, M. Paniagua, A. Ben-Ari, E. Pretto, S. Eisdorfer, E. Davidson, I Matot, & C. Eisdorfer. (2007). Uncomplicated general anesthesia in the elderly results in cognitive decline: Does cognitive decline predict morbidity and mortality? Medical Hypotheses, 68:3, 484-492.

Megré, V. (2002). The Book of Kin. The Ringing Cedar Series • Book Six. Kahului, Hawaii: Ringing Cedars Press.

Miller, F. & D. Meier. (1998). Voluntary death: A comparison of terminal dehydration and physician-assisted suicide. Annals of Internal Medicine 128:7, 559-562.

Parnia, S. (2006). What happens when we die: A groundbreaking study into the nature of life and death. Carlsbad, CA: Hay House, Inc.

Rinpoche, G., Fremantle, F. & Trungpa, C. (translators). (1987). The Tibetan book of the dead: The great liberation through hearing in the Bardo. Boston: Shambhala Dragon Editions

Ruiz, D. (1997). The Four Agreements. San Rafael, CA: Amber-Allen Publishing.

Schneider, P. & G. Pieroth. (1998). Light beings - Master essences. Twin Lakes, WI: Arcana Publishing.

Schroeder-Sheker, T. (2001). Transitus: A blessed death in the modern world. St. Dunstan's Press

Self, J. (2009). The shift. www.MasteringAlchemy.com

Stewart, D. (2010). Healing oils of the bible. Marble Hill, MO: Care Publications.

Stone, J.D. (1994). The complete ascension manual: How to achieve ascension in this Lifetime. Flaggstaff, AZ: Light Technology Publishing.

Tomer, A., G. Eliason, & P. Wong (Eds). (2008). Existential and spiritual issues in death attitudes. New York, NY: Taylor & Francis Group, LLC.

Walsch, N.D. (2006). Home with God: In a life that never ends. New York, NY: Atria Books

Weidner, J. (Ed). (2009). Infinity: the ultimate trip. Journey beyond death. (Film) Ashland, OR: Sacred Mysteries Productions.

Weissman, D. (2005). The power of infinite love & gratitude: An evolutionary journey to awakening your spirit. Carlsbad, CA: Hay House.

Willis-Brandon, C. (2000). One last hug before I go: The mystery and meaning of deathbed visions. Deerfield Beach, FL: Health Communications, Inc.

Worwood, V.A. (1999). Aromatherapy for the soul: Healing the spirit with fragrance and essential oils. Novato, CA: New World Library.

Index

A

abdominal breathing (energy breathing), 132
Abraham-Hicks, 16
acceptance, hospice team and, 26
advocate, 21, 23, 26
affirmation, 50, 57, 61, 64, 73, 75, 77, 78, 88
afterlife, 3
agitation, 40, 50, 62–63
Alzheimer's disease, 8, 22–24, 43, 109–114
Amazing Power of Deliberate Intent, The (Hicks), 99
Anastasia, 48
angels, 3, 5, 38, 52, 138
anoint, 50, 54, 59–60, 80, 84, 122, 123, 127
Anointing of the Sick Sacrament, 45
anxiety, 1, 17, 26, 40, 44, 50, 102, 110
appreciation, 57, 119
aromatherapy, 122–123
astral plane, 30–31, 49, 51
Ativan, 40, 46
Atwater, P. M. H., 3, 21–22, 96
aura, 30, 53, 60, 123
Ave Maria (Shubert), 55–56, 79, 90, 126

B

Bardo, 7, 49, 54, 67–69, 80, 84
Bibliography, 96, 141–144
birthing, 61
body of the self, 38–39
Book of Kin, The (Megré), 48
Braden, Gregg, 106, 118–119
breathing techniques, 15
breathwork, 35–36, 39, 48–49, 60–61, 73, 75, 77
Brinkley, Dannion, 135
Buddhism, 38
Butler, Robert, 101–102

C

CDs, 15, 55, 140
chakra cleanse and illumination, 60, 78, 128–130
chakras, 60, 73, 77–78, 123, 128–130
chantrum, 55
Christ consciousness, 56, 59, 105–106
Cocoon Meditation, 110–112
cognitive decline, 8, 23, 27
coherency, 119–120
commitments, 95
Communion, 13, 56, 61
compassion, hospice team and, 26
Complete Ascension Manual, The (Stone), 54, 122
consciousness, 35, 38, 48, 68, 88, 105
cremation, 7, 84–85
crown chakra, 54, 60, 61, 74, 125, 128

D

Dale, Cyndi, 105
deathbed promises, 95–96
deathbed visions (DBV), 3, 10, 96
dehydration, 25, 115–116
delirium, 40, 57
dementia, 31, 103, 120
depression, 1, 8, 11, 14, 17
Dilaudid, 46, 60, 72
dimension, 56, 81, 89, 117
Divine Matrix, 61, 106, 118–119
Divine Mother-Father God, 36, 47, 48, 61, 131–132
dowsing, 124
dreams, 11, 17, 28, 102
Dyer, Wayne, 99

E

earth plane, 53
ecumenical minister, 59
eighth chakra, 129–130
electromagnetic energy field, 119
emotions, 16–17, 26, 49, 67, 105, 107, 121
Emoto, Masaru, 107
end-of-life care, 101
end-of-life review, 71–72, 102–103, 134–135
energy, 2, 10, 18, 23, 29–30, 46–49, 53, 56, 61–63, 80, 89–90, 105, 112
entrainment, 119–120
esoteric, 87, 89
essence, 38–39
Essene, 39
essential oils, 52, 54, 122–123
ethics, 95
Eucharist, 56

F

fear, 1, 9, 26, 56, 105–106, 109–110
Five Wishes, 99–104
forgiveness, 30, 50, 103–104
Four Agreements, The (Ruiz), 109
frankincense, 54

G

Gandi, Mohandas, xi
geranium essential oil, 53
Gibran, Kahlil, 86, 88
Global Coherence Initiative (GCI), 120
God, 5, 10, 15–16, 36, 44–45, 61–63, 131
God is Light, 68
grace, 38, 50, 60, 61, 70, 81–82
gratitude, 30, 36, 57, 64, 73, 84, 108, 113–114
Great Liberation Through Hearing, The, 67
grief, 35, 49, 56, 63, 114
grounding cord, 132–133
guided imagery, 15

H

Hail Mary, 15, 44, 48, 61
Hail Mary, Gentle Woman, 48, 65–66, 70, 80, 85
harmony, 23, 49, 59–78
Hawkins, David, 105–106
heart chakra, 69, 74, 81, 125
heaven, 4, 10, 35, 45, 71
Hicks, Esther and Jerry, 99
Hidden Messages in Water, The (Emoto), 107
Higher Self, 17, 29, 124, 125, 136
hip fractures, 22
hologram, 48, 119
holotropic breathwork, 35, 37–38
Holy Spirit, 52, 74
home, 3, 10, 14–19, 71, 74, 81–82, 117–127
Home with God: In a Life that Never Ends (Walsch), 9, 11, 28
hospice, 25–26, 39, 41, 43–45, 72–73, 114
hospice team, 25–27, 37, 39, 41
hospital, 20–21, 34–35, 37, 41–42, 46, 51–52
Houston, Jean, 31

I

imagination, 76–77, 110
Inca, 60, 128
incense, 52
indigenous people, 52, 118
Infinite Love and Gratitude, 107–108, 114

Infinity: The Ultimate Trip.
  Journey Beyond Death,
  135
initiation, 39, 74
In-patient Unit (IPU), 43, 44,
  46
Institute of HeartMath,
  119–120
Intensol, 46, 72
intention, 99–104
Into the Light, 79–82
Intuition, 32, 51, 123
invocation, 47, 53, 62, 131

J

japa, 73
Jesus, 30
John 1, 4:8, 68
John 1, 1:5, 68
journal, 103
journey, 7, 60–61, 74
joy, 59–78

K

kinesiology, 106, 124
Kubler-Ross, Elizabeth, 3
Kwan Yin, 52, 80

L

Landry, Carey, 66
Law of Attraction, 16, 106
Law of Vibration, 106
Lerma, John, 97, 117

life cycle, 64, 87–88
life review, 12, 101–104,
  134–135
Light, 4, 6, 10, 30, 42, 50–53,
  56, 79–82
limiting belief, 17, 110
Living Will, 43
*Lokah Samastah Sukhino
  Bhavantu* (Hindu prayer),
  73
lotus flower, 38
love, 26, 59–78
Lucia, Lucy, 88–91
Luminous Energy Field, 30

M

mandala, 35–36, 38
Mary Magdalene, 52, 80
Mass, 10–11, 85
meditation, 7, 37, 39,
  110–112, 120
memory book, 103
metaphor, 33, 64
metaphysical tools, 52, 110,
  120–121, 132
Moody, Raymond, 97, 102
Mother Earth, 53, 64, 113,
  118, 124–125, 132–133
mudra, 107, 114
multidimensional, 35–36,
  61–68
music, 55, 62, 76–77, 90,
  106–107, 120

music-thanatology, 76–77
mystical journey, 7

N
Native Americans, 52
near-death experiences (NDE), 3, 10, 98, 102
negative and positive energy, 13, 47, 51–53, 120–121
non-judgmental listener, 103
number 13, 79, 87
number3, 87–88
numerology, 79, 87

O
Om Mani Padma Hum (Tibetan Buddhism mantra), 38
orange light, 54

P
pain, 14–15, 22–23, 62–63, 109–114
pain management, 21, 26, 43–44, 46, 72
Palo Santo, 52
peace, 59–78
Peace & Calming®, 66
pendulum, 123–127, 132–133
permission, 17, 49, 57, 91, 106, 128
Power of Attorney (POA), 8, 21, 35, 39, 72

Power of Infinite Love and Gratitude, The (Weissman), 107–108, 114
Power of Intention, The (Dyer), 99
Power vs. Force: The Hidden Determinants of Human Behavior (Hawkins), 105
pray, 15, 68
prayer, 7, 30, 38, 44–45, 48–49, 65–66, 68–70, 73, 84–86, 118–119
pre-death experiences, 3–5, 52, 96, 97
Prophet, The (Gibran), 86
purgatory, 15, 16, 17
purification, 15–16

Q
quality of care, 26–27, 44
quantum hologram, 118–119
quantum physics, 106

R
rainbow body, 60, 128
rainbow bridge, 36
rebirth, 22
recapitulation, 102
Reiki, 18, 29, 52, 56
Reiki Phowa, 7, 30, 54, 140
Ringing Cedar Series, The, 48

ritual, 61, 65, 68–69, 70, 79–80, 95–96
root chakra, 64, 77–78, 129, 130
Rosary, 15, 59, 68, 70
Rosa's Radiant Transition, xiii
Rose Energy Tool, 110, 112–114
rose flower essence, 69–70
roses, 69, 112
Ruiz, Don Miguel, 109

S

sacral chakra, 130
sacred space, 46–58, 61, 62, 66
sadness, 21, 35, 90
sage, 52
sandalwood, 53, 122
Self, Jim, 16–17
self-limiting beliefs, 18
shamanic, 60
shanti, shanti, shanti (mantra), 73
shell, 111–112
Shift, The (Self e-book), 16–17
sign language, 107
sludge, 128
smudge, 52
solar plexus chakra, 130

soul, 10, 17, 29, 30–31, 39, 51, 59–60, 74–75, 81–82, 83–84, 124
soul transitioning, 75–76
Source, 131
spark of God, 38–39
Speaking the Lost Language of God, 118
spiritual being, 5, 30, 52, 69, 72
spiritual realm, 68, 135
spritzed, 52
Stone, Joshua David, 54, 122
subconscious, 17, 55, 110, 123, 124
subtle energy, 7, 52, 54–55, 124, 136
suffering, 15, 51, 72, 109
sweet grass, 52

T

Tarot, 87, 88
terminal dehydration, 115–116
third eye chakra, 54, 130
thoughts, 14, 16–17, 100, 105–108, 119, 124
throat chakra, 81
Tibetan, 30, 38
Tibetan Book of the Dead, 7, 67
touch, 26, 72, 119

tranquility, 55–56
transgressions, 50, 67, 103
transition, 1–7, 46–58, 79–82, 102–104

U

Unconditional Love, 56, 59, 81–82, 111
understanding, 26, 35, 48
Universal Field of Oneness, 56, 131
universal laws, 106

V

Vedas, 49
Vedic teachings, 51
veil, 3, 5, 10, 81
vibration, 16–18, 49, 54–57, 70, 105–108
vibrational energy, 16, 54, 56, 73, 105–108, 112–113

Victim Triangle, 95
violet flame, 53, 118, 120–121
visualizations, 15, 64
vortex, 53, 67, 84, 118

W

Walsch, Neal Donald, 9, 28, 135
Weissman, Darren, 107
We Live Forever: The Real Truth About Death (Atwater), 21–22
Where love is, there is God also, xi
White Angelica™, 52–53, 122
Worwood, V., 54

Y

Young Living, 52–53, 66